Self-Made in America

Self-Made

JOHN McCORMACK

with David R. Legge

Addison-Wesley Publishing Company

in America

Plain Talk for Plain People about the Meaning of Success

Reading, Massachusetts   Menlo Park, California   New York

Don Mills, Ontario   Wokingham, England   Amsterdam   Bonn

Sydney   Singapore   Tokyo   Madrid   San Juan

Paris   Seoul   Milan   Mexico City   Taipei

"What It Takes to Be No. 1" by Vince Lombardi, copyright © 1990, is repro-
duced with permission of the Estate of Vince Lombardi. Authorized by Curtis
Management Group, Indianapolis, Indiana, USA.

"The Touch of the Master's Hand" by Myra Brooks Welch, copyright © 1952
The Touch of the Master's Hand by Brethen Press, is reprinted by special
permission of Brethren Press.

Many of the designations used by manufacturers and sellers to distinguish
their products are claimed as trademarks. Where those designations appear
in this book and Addison-Wesley was aware of a trademark claim, the designations have been printed in initial capital letters (e.g., Rolex).

Library of Congress Cataloging-in-Publication Data

McCormack, John, 1944-
    Self-made in America : plain talk for plain people about
    the meaning of success / John McCormack with David R. Legge.
        p.   cm.
    Includes index.
    ISBN 0-201-55099-7
    ISBN 0-201-60823-5 (pbk.)
    1. Success in business—United States.   I. Legge, David R.
    II. Title.
    HF5386.M4738   1991
    650.1—dc20   90-43883
                                                        CIP

Copyright © 1990 by The Visible Changes Educational Founda-
tion and David R. Legge

Jacket design by Mike Stromberg
Text design by Barbara Werden
Set in 10-point Waldbaum by World Composition Services, Inc., Sterling, VA

10 11 12 13 14-MA-0099989796
Tenth printing, September 1996

To the American people, and especially our hardworking new immigrants who are re-teaching us the dreams, visions, and lessons that made our country great.

To God, for allowing me to be human and make mistakes while always giving me the perseverance and wisdom to know when He was showing me where to find the knowledge and power to solve the problems.

In memory of my mom, who had the insight to write in my grammar school graduation book the following quote:

> *"John,*
> *Always remember that every tragedy in our life is a test of our faith. Therefore the answer always will come from God."*

Contents

Foreword

I have read hundreds of business books. Quite simply, I believe this book, *Self-Made in America,* is one of the finest books ever written.

More to the point, John McCormack's masterpiece is a must-read, not only for every business person, but for his or her spouse, children, employees, and associates. The information is *that* important and timely. I include children—at least middle-school-age and older—because young people need to know what it takes to become truly successful in America. One wonderful feature is that John, along with his cowriter, David R. Legge, has made *Self-Made* so down-to-earth and easy to understand. At the same time, they have filled the pages with colorful stories and action plans, making it difficult for readers to put it down.

Frankly, I like *Self-Made in America* because I can relate to John McCormack. We have similar backgrounds. We are both New York kids who grew up with a desire to accomplish something worthwhile. It took both of us several entrepreneurial attempts and years of hard times before we made the choices which carried us to success. I enjoy the way he speaks and writes, for it is apparent to anyone that John is brimming over with a fiery desire to bring positive changes to the world. Above all, I respect the author of this book because he's an extraordinary dreamer and remarkable achiever. Anyone with his track record deserves all the admiration in the world.

Therefore, when I talk about how much I believe in John and his message, I have practiced what I continue to preach. I've bought hundreds of copies. I've given them to each of my seven children. I've handed them out to other family members, friends, and acquaintances. I've even given them to waitpersons, mechanics, store clerks, and other people with whom I do business regularly—especially when those men and women express an honest curiosity about what it takes to make it in life. In addition, I've distributed thousands and thousands of copies to my business associates throughout the United States and around the globe.

Why?

In the opening passages, John warns, "The fundamentals you will learn in this book work *only if you work*." Near the final page, he writes, "The purpose of this book never was to make success look easy for you. It was to make success *possible* for you."

In between, the battle-seasoned author helps readers understand the unvarnished laws of success, then he offers time-proven applications and tools for accomplishing great things. Using his words, John has written "plain talk for plain people about the meaning of success."

What could be better?

Enjoy the pages. Properly understood and implemented, the profound lessons from John McCormack's *Self-Made in America* will change your life forever!

—Dexter R. Yager, Sr.
Financial, business, and
marketing consultant

Acknowledgments

As flattering as the title of this book is, of course, no man or woman is *Self-Made in America,* and I've been fortunate to have more than my share of help along the way. Specifically, I'd like to thank:

Joe and Millie Biancaniello, for teaching me at a very young age the importance of communication between parents and children.

Frank Crimmins, for telling me I was selling myself short by remaining a cop. Abe, Nick, and Bernie and all the rest of the entrepreneurs I have studied under.

At Visible Changes, Cleta Gordon Logan, Cheryl Bradford, Sandi Morton, Carl Fairman, and all our staff members, without whose ideas and input this book would never be on the bookshelf.

Special thanks to Don Weckwerth, the banker, and David Stovall, the accountant, who believed in the dream before it became a reality.

Also to Vince Lombardi, Ray Kroc, and Walt Disney, who have shown us all that the reality can become even bigger than the dream.

To my brother, Joe, who along with me has been battling the problems of life with ADD and never allowed it to beat us.

On a more personal note, special thanks and thoughts to my three children for whom I hope this book becomes the cornerstone for *their* future.

And lastly, I want to thank especially the person who believed in me all the time, even when I didn't believe in myself, Maryanne.

—John McCormack

Acknowledgments

Into every writer's life, an editor or two must fall, and on this project I've been fortunate to work with that rare breed of editor whose sensitivity, experience, and, yes, wisdom have made this a far better book than it otherwise would have been.

Specifically, I'd like to thank Jane Isay for helping us shape this manuscript, Lisa Crystal for doing a superhuman copy-editing job, and Laura Noorda, our production supervisor, without whom this book might have been published a year or two from now.

Sandra Dijkstra, our agent, was always there for us, and it was such a pleasure to work with a literary agent who is actually literate herself.

And, first, last, and always, I want to thank Vicki Butler for all of her hard work, sound advice, and endless encouragement on this project. Along the way, Vicki taught me how beautiful a person can be, on the inside as well as the outside.

—David R. Legge

Introduction

by David R. Legge

COMEDIAN ROBIN WILLIAMS tells a wonderful story about a man who lapses into deep sleep and dreams of two visions for his son.

In Vision No. 1, the son enters a hushed, hallowed hall full of distinguished guests, steps upon the stage, and approaches the microphone. After clearing his throat, the young man begins: "First, I want to thank the Nobel Prize Committee for this high honor. . . ."

In Vision No. 2, the same son steps up to a counter and asks with a quiver in his voice, "You want fries with that order? . . ."

The difference between these two possible scenarios for the same young man is what this book is all about. Our storyteller, John McCormack, has lived both lives: that of the down-and-out loser and the supremely successful entrepreneur.

Before I pass the podium to John to begin his tale, I want to share with you the circumstances under which I first met McCormack.

About two years ago, I received a call asking me to serve on a committee of the Houston Chamber of Commerce that intended to recognize the most innovative companies in Houston.

Houston, in addition to being known as an international city and the capital of the "oil bidness," also likes to think of itself as the last bastion of capitalism in the country. This is a city run by businessmen, for businessmen. It's been called the last refuge of scalawags and scoundrels who came up one ace short at the poker table or one wife too many in a motel room and had to leave their last town—well, in a hurry.

Houston, in a sense, embodies the most basic belief of the American dream: it's a first-chance city, where people can start up—or a last-chance city, where people can start over. In fact, the lore of Houston is replete with roll-the-dice stories of men and women who bet the farm—and the future—on little more than a good idea and a lot of guts. It is the perfect city for entrepreneurs, and many have made many millions here.

Nevertheless, at the time we were putting together nominees for the most innovative companies, Houston itself had been coming up an ace or two short in the economic poker game. With the worldwide collapse of oil prices, Houston—where more than 50 percent of the economy is based to one degree or another on the price of a barrel of oil—was just emerging from a three-year depression.

The city, known for its boom in the seventies, became known for its bust in the eighties. Beautiful, modernistic downtown skyscrapers were empty. Everything was for sale. Pawnbrokers couldn't peddle the glut of gold Rolex watches they had loaned money on. The only people who had more business than they could handle were the bankruptcy lawyers.

And so, to add a little light to this darkness, the Greater Houston Chamber of Commerce decided to do a little cheerleading and pat a few companies on the back.

All in all, we examined perhaps 150 companies to come up with, eventually, one winner in each of the following three categories: People, Products, and Processes. After we had whittled the field down to nine (three in each category), someone got the idea that we had better interview the owners or chief executives of these companies to be sure they weren't operating out of a telephone booth or a post office box number.

John McCormack, who owned an extremely successful chain of sixteen hair salons in Texas called "Visible Changes," was a finalist in the People category. His company had not only survived the Houston depression, it had flourished, establishing record

Introduction

year after record year of increased sales, profits, and personal successes, culminating in 1988 with McCormack's being on the cover of *Inc.* magazine, featured as "The Hottest Entrepreneur in America."

I called George Gendron, the editor of *Inc.* magazine and a longtime friend, to ask him about McCormack. "He's the real thing," reported Gendron. "The guy's phenomenal."

I then called McCormack to inform him of his impending honor, and he agreed to give me thirty minutes. That first meeting, which was one of our shortest to date, lasted four hours.

Although I had been a journalist for more than twenty years (at *The Washington Post, Newsweek,* etc.), and had spent time with people ranging from mass murderers to presidents to kings, I had never met anyone as mesmerizing as McCormack.

I was reminded of one of my favorite quotes from Jack Kerouac's classic novel, *On the Road:* "The only people for me are the mad ones, the ones who are mad to live, mad to talk, mad to be saved, desirous of everything at the same time, the ones who never yawn or say a commonplace thing, but burn, burn, burn like fabulous yellow Roman candles exploding like spiders across the stars and in the middle you see the blue centerlight pop and everybody goes 'Awww!' "—and on and on in breathless, tireless, teletype prose. That was McCormack.

Like many of his Irish forebears, McCormack is a storyteller, and in this book, he'll introduce you to some of the most memorable characters you're ever likely to meet. There's Abe, his mentor, who, at age seventy-five, snookered him into a hundred-yard race for fifty bucks. There's Bernie, the Yiddish-speaking immigrant, who peddled "vashing machines" up and down Delancey Street in New York City before building an empire worth millions of dollars today. And then there's Nick, who, to this day, will tell you he "rolls meatballs" for his millions a year. Nick got on the wrong boat to come to America—it was headed for South America—and spent some time crisscrossing the Atlantic as a merchant seaman, eventually jumping ship into the icy January waters of Philadelphia harbor without a dollar in his pocket or a word of English in his vocabulary.

Nearly all of McCormack's close friends and business associates share a common heritage: they are all immigrants who came to this country with nothing—and today, they are all multimillionaires. They taught McCormack how they became successful *starting with nothing,* and, in this book, McCormack is going to teach you how you too can become successful, regardless of your educational background, work experience, or present position in life.

Be warned and be prepared: This is no namby-pamby textbook on entrepreneurial theory that you might find at the Harvard Business School or Stanford University. Think of this more as a guerrilla-warfare guide to business and life, written by someone business-wise, street-smart, and cop-tough.

McCormack was raised in a Queens, New York, town called Queens Village. He lived in an Archie Bunker–type house and was told repeatedly by his father that he'd never amount to anything. He began to believe it himself, just barely making it, in his words, "out the back door of my high school with a diploma." For generations, the male McCormacks had gone into one of two professions: the priesthood or the police force.

"Since celibacy was out of the question," says McCormack, "I became a New York City cop."

For three years McCormack explored the underbelly of New York low life: drug dealers, prostitutes, and kids who would as soon kill you as look at you. Forty-second Street, Eighth Avenue, the South Bronx, the whole mess. For eighty-one dollars a week. That was twenty years ago.

Today, along with his wife Maryanne, McCormack owns Visi-

Introduction

ble Changes, a computer software company, a products company, and substantial real estate holdings. He and his wife take seven-figure salaries from Visible Changes, and, although they own 100 percent of their company, each year the staff vote on whether they stay or go (corporate CEOs take note). They recently moved into their new million-dollar home (*Inc.* magazine made a big deal over the fact that it had twelve bathrooms), which McCormack himself designed—to the dismay of his builder—on the backs of paper bags and other scraps of paper.

McCormack, whose customary fee is ten thousand dollars to deliver a two-hour talk, last year received more than two hundred invitations to address various groups on how he and his company have achieved their phenomenal success. Some of the major graduate schools of business in America, including UCLA, Wharton, Notre Dame, the University of Texas, and Rice, are coming to this high school graduate for counsel on how to prepare their students to succeed, not in the artificial environment of the classroom, but in the rough-and-tumble environment of the real world.

Many Fortune 500 companies, such as IBM and J.C. Penney, are studying McCormack's techniques in motivation and compensation, and his ability to build not just successful companies but companies full of successful people.

What McCormack has done for the haircutting industry has been likened to what Ray Kroc did for the hamburger industry when he founded McDonald's. Just look at some numbers:

- An "average" hair salon in America takes in about $150,000 per year in sales. An average Visible Changes salon does more than a million a year, and most are in the $1.5 million to $2 million range.
- An "average" haircutter in America makes about $12,000 per year. Haircutters at Visible Changes make on average

$33,000, many are in the $50,000 to $70,000 range, and a few are earning nearly $100,000.

What makes McCormack's success all the more remarkable is that it's not just a business success; it's a *people* success. Think for a moment. Who becomes a hairdresser in America? Usually single women with less than a high school education who become pregnant before they're eighteen, job hoppers—or men who are assumed to be gay. They don't earn enough money to provide the basic amenities for their families, and generally are thought of as losers or rejects, first by society, second by their parents, and third by themselves.

McCormack recruits from this same labor pool, but he turns losers into winners, winners into stars, and, in many cases, stars into superstars. McCormack's staff—and he's got about five hundred of them—have turned their lives around. They've got pride, self-esteem, and money in the bank. (An average American saves less than 5 percent of his or her income. McCormack's people save more than 40 percent.) In most cases, the women hold off having babies until, one, they have a husband, and two, they can afford to support a family. The company is virtually drug free and theft free. The staff love their jobs and, probably for the first time in their lives, appear to love themselves.

How has McCormack accomplished all this when the public schools and even the families of his people have failed so miserably? That's what this book is all about. McCormack believes that anybody can turn his or her life around and become a success at any age, regardless of education or past failures. Ray Kroc, he likes to point out, didn't get started with McDonald's until his mid-fifties, when he was in such bad health that he couldn't even obtain personal medical insurance. By age seventy, he had forever changed American business and, more important, the lives of thousands upon thousands of McDonald's franchisees.

Introduction

In these pages, McCormack will teach you the fundamentals of success that he learned, ironically, from studying under immigrants.

- He'll introduce you to the "20 Percent Rule," whereby you must live on just 20 percent of your income, regardless of your salary, and put the other 80 percent into savings.
- He'll share with you the golden rule of entrepreneurship: "When in doubt, trust thyself." McCormack believes that entrepreneurs must look within themselves to find the strength to go on—when all the world is telling them to go back, to quit, that they don't stand a chance.
- He'll tell you stories, both personal and of his friends, which give new meaning to the phrase "whatever it takes." McCormack himself was rejected by 299 banks before he finally found a banker who believed in him (even though the banker had grave doubts about the potential of Visible Changes). Walt Disney, McCormack likes to point out, was turned down by 302 banks before he hit the jackpot.
- And above all, by his own example, McCormack will convince you that if he can become a multimillionaire in America, anyone can—including yourself.

This book, then, in its simplest form, is a road map to success. On this road map there are no detours and no shortcuts. If you're willing to do "whatever it takes," this book tells you, in a tough, no-nonsense way, exactly what it takes.

The fundamentals you will read about, McCormack emphasizes, apply whether you are a business school graduate or a grammar school dropout, a fledgling entrepreneur or a corporate executive.

If this book, at times, sounds simple, or even simplistic, it is simply because success is simple, if we adhere to a few fundamentals with which most of us are already equipped. Where we stumble along the road to success in our business and personal lives is in the *application* of these fundamentals that we already know or possess or can easily be taught.

This book, therefore, begins with an explanation of what these fundamentals are, illustrated first anecdotally by McCormack's experience with successful mentors, specifically Abe, Bernie, and Nick.

Importantly and ironically, the fundamentals that McCormack learned from his foreign friends were once thought to be uniquely American (truth, honesty, commitment, persistence, self-discipline, hard work, a day's pay for a day's work, etc.) but have largely disappeared from the American landscape over a period of post World War II permissiveness brought on by material success and personal indulgence. In effect, McCormack believes Americans have become mentally lazy and physically flabby.

At the beginning of each chapter, McCormack will emphasize a key lesson to be learned or an exercise to be performed. He will then share some personal experiences which illustrate that fundamental in practice. Finally, in closing each chapter, he will summarize the key points covered.

The good news is that if you adhere to the few fundamentals you will read about in these pages, you will become whatever you dream you can be. It's paradoxical (but true) that *theorizing* about success is complex but easy, while *doing* something about success is simple but difficult. The fundamentals you will learn in this book work *only if you work.*

At the close of our initial four-hour meeting and after hearing I was a writer, McCormack acknowledged that he had been approached by no fewer than a dozen writers who wanted to do his book, but that he wasn't yet ready to set aside the necessary time. In subsequent meetings, I attempted to convince him that his

Introduction

message was too important not to be shared with a nation that is rapidly falling behind the rest of the world in both industry and education, as well as deteriorating badly both economically and socially.

After several more meetings (I was learning persistence, in part from him), McCormack agreed to commit the time, resources, and effort necessary to make this book a reality.

One footnote: When John and Maryanne started Visible Changes 13 years ago, they gave their first profits of $106,000 back to their staff. At a recent company conference—an annual gala black-tie affair for about seven hundred invitees—McCormack announced that he was establishing a foundation to fund education for the children of his staff. To kick it off, he was writing a personal check for $106,000 to match the first contribution. He also pledged to contribute all of his profits and royalties from this book to the education fund.

(P.S.: Yes, McCormack got the Chamber of Commerce award.)

Part One

Learning the Laws
of Success

Chapter 1

Getting Naked

DENIAL. ASK ANY psychologist what the major obstacle to recovery is, and the likely response will be denial. It's fundamental. Until you admit there is a problem, you can't begin to solve it. Likewise, until you can identify the strengths and weaknesses that are uniquely yours, you can't begin to take advantage of your opportunities.

Therefore, in this chapter, we will concentrate on putting together an honest self-examination or "personal balance sheet." I call this exercise "getting naked"—looking in the mirror and asking yourself, "Could anyone fall in love with that?" I promise you, the balance sheet you will construct is unlike any other you've ever put down on paper. Once it's down in black and white, denial is impossible.

Before we get to that, however, I want to begin with the premise that America as a nation, its leaders as well as its people, is in a state of collective denial. We still think of ourselves as the land of the free and the home of the brave. The cradle of democracy. The nation with the highest living standard in the world. And on and on.

The facts, however, belie the platitudes, and I'm here to tell you at the outset that I believe America is in deep trouble as a nation. We have lost our will to win and our ability to compete. Let's look at a cursory national balance sheet:

In less than a decade, we have gone from being the largest creditor nation to the largest debtor nation in the world. Among industrialized countries, America ranks first in drug use, divorce, murder, rape, illegitimate children, infant mortality, teenage pregnancy, the trade deficit, and national debt.

In our last congressional elections, there was less turnover in the House of Representatives than there was in the Soviet Politburo: 98 percent of the incumbents were reelected! Among developed nations, America ranks last in workplace productivity and next to last in literacy and education.

A recent Barbara Walters television special, "America's Kids: Why They Flunk," showed that:

- Fewer than half of America's high school seniors had ever heard of apartheid or the greenhouse effect, and nearly 70 percent could not identify Chernobyl as the worst nuclear accident in history. One student thought "Chernobyl" was Cher's full name.

- Only half of the high school seniors could locate Washington D.C., the nation's capital, on a world map. It showed up in Nicaragua, France, and Egypt.

- In a Gallup Poll designed to measure what Americans know, it turns out that in the supposedly "best-educated nation on earth," we know practically nothing. Plato was identified as Mickey Mouse's dog, his counterpart Aristotle was identified as Jacqueline Kennedy Onassis's husband, and the most important Flemish painter of the seventeenth century, Peter Paul Rubens, was identified as, you guessed it, a corned beef sandwich.

- Two-thirds of all students spend less than one hour per day on homework and between three and five hours in front of the television set, watching music videos, cartoons, and other mind mush. In fact, the literacy rate is so low in America that Chrysler chairman Lee Iacocca recently reported that so many of his assembly-line workers couldn't read the simple words "bad hood fit" on a quality control button that he had to replace the words with a graphic depiction. Said Iacocca, "If you don't have people who are smarter than the robots they work with, the game is over."

Getting Naked

In my experience, most of the people I meet in business put in fewer than twenty real hours of hard work per week. Of course I'm subtracting the long lunches, the interminable meetings, and the busywork that passes for work in so much of American business today. America, in just a decade or two, appears to have lost its ability to compete and its will to win.

Vince Lombardi, the great coach of the Green Bay Packers who is perhaps identified more with winning than any other American folk hero, used to be fond of saying that he would gladly share his playbook with the opposing team before the game. The secret to winning, he said, wasn't in looking at a series of plays on a sheet of paper, but in executing them. Keep it simple, Lombardi said, and master the fundamentals.

In recent years, I've printed thousands of posters of Vince Lombardi's credo for success, and I'd like to share it with you, as I have with my distributors, friends, and associates. It's also on the walls of all of our salons, and it's entitled,

What It Takes to Be No. 1

Winning is not a sometime thing; it's an all-the-time thing. You don't win once in a while. You don't do things right once in a while. You do them right all the time. Winning is a habit. Unfortunately, so is losing.

There is no room for second place. There is only one place in my game and that is first place. I have finished second twice in my time at Green Bay, and I don't ever want to finish second again. There is a second place bowl game, but it is a game for losers played by losers. It is and always has been American zeal to be first in anything we do and to win and to win and to win.

Every time a football player goes out to ply his trade, he's got to play from the ground up—from the soles of his feet right up to his head. Every inch of him has to play.

Some guys play with their heads. That's okay. You've got to be smart to be No. 1 in any business. But more important, you've got to play with your heart—with every fiber of your body. If you're lucky enough to find a guy with a lot of head and a lot of heart, he's never going to come off the field second.

Running a football team is no different from running any other kind of organization—an army, a political party, a business. The principles are the same. The object is to win—to beat the other guy. Maybe that sounds hard or cruel. I don't think it is.

It's a reality of life that men are competitive and the most competitive games draw the most competitive men. That's why they're there—to compete. They know the rules and the objectives when they get in the game. The objective is to win—fairly, squarely, decently, by the rules—but to win.

And in truth, I've never known a man worth his salt who in the long run, deep down in his heart, didn't appreciate the grind, the discipline. There is something in good men that really yearns for—needs—discipline and the harsh reality of head-to-head combat.

I don't say these things because I believe in the "brute" nature of man or that men must be brutalized to be combative. I believe in God, and I believe in human decency. But I firmly believe that any man's finest hour—his greatest fulfillment to all he holds dear—is that moment when he has worked his heart out in a good cause and lies exhausted on the field of battle—victorious.

Lombardi was tough, for sure, but so is football, so is business, and, in fact, so is life. President Bush has said he wants "a kinder

Getting Naked

and gentler America." I'm more inclined to go along with Senator Robert Dole, who says he wants a "rougher and tougher America."

I now want to share with you the circumstances that led me to my own brutally honest inward look. I think it was columnist George F. Will who wrote of Joe DiMaggio's selling "Mr. Coffee" machines on television that "you have to rise so high in order to fall so low." Likewise, by age twenty-four I was more than a millionaire and by age twenty-five I was out of work, a quarter of a million dollars in debt, and considering suicide. Let me briefly tell you about the rise—and fall—of John McCormack:

After high school I became a tough billy-club-across-the-backside New York cop with a wise-guy attitude and an eighty-one-dollar-a-week paycheck.

We were tough cops then, and it's a good thing, because those were tough times, the sixties, when race riots were rampant in America. My first beat was Brooklyn and soon after that, Harlem, the war zone. I remember going to one riot in a police car, and, just after I got out, someone pushing a refrigerator off the top of a building, sending it through the roof of my police car like a torpedo. My partner looked at me and said, "Well, we were lucky today."

In Harlem, if the bad guys wanted to shoot you, they'd just shoot. They didn't really care. The badge to them was little more than a target. The concept of law and order was a joke. Anybody who hasn't been there has no idea of how bad it was—and is. I worked the streets for three years.

One time I was assigned to a single-person radio car, cruising the back streets of Jamaica in Queens. I received a call about a robbery in progress at a bodega—a deli for Spanish people. I went racing to the scene, passing at full speed two cop cars heading toward the holdup as if they were on a leisurely Sunday drive.

I pulled my car in front of the building, pulled out my gun, and found myself face to face with three guys running out of the building. They had shotguns.

I was both outmanned and outgunned, so I decided that talking was better than shooting. I very conspicuously put my gun back into the holster. I told them that the place was surrounded and to drop their guns. "Now!"

One of the guys said, "Shoot him."

I continued: "If you shoot me, I promise you, you'll fry. Now, if you give up, I'll tell the judge that you cooperated, and you'll be out before I finish my paperwork. How much money did you get out of this dump anyway?"

The lead guy said, "Twenty-seven dollars. Yeah, you're right, man." They threw down their guns, and the confrontation was over before it started.

When I got back to the station, I started to do some overdue serious thinking. "I'm going to put my life on the line for someone else's twenty-seven bucks? These animals don't understand me, and I don't understand them. I've got to start looking for something else."

The holidays were near and I had about two weeks of vacation time coming, so I thought I would make a few extra bucks selling Christmas trees with my brother, also a New York City cop. I talked the owner of a vacant lot into letting us use his property in exchange for cutting down the tall weeds that had him in trouble with the city.

My brother and I pooled our wealth and scraped together three hundred dollars—enough to buy one truckload of trees. Only a couple hours into opening day, however, we encountered our first crisis in the business world: we learned that most New Yorkers bought their trees after work, that is to say, after dark, and we, of course, had no lights or even electricity on our lot. "We're out of business," my brother said. "It was a dumb idea anyway. After all, we're cops, not Christmas tree salesmen. Let's go home."

Getting Naked

Well, we didn't go home. We had already cleared the weeds and paid for the trees. Eventually it dawned on us that the only thing between our lights and somebody's electricity was a long, very long, extension cord—which we proceeded to buy.

Then we started knocking on doors, asking if we could "borrow a plug." After a dozen or so noes, we finally met a woman who invited us in from the cold and listened to our hard-luck story. By chance, she had a son who also was a New York City cop. After finishing our hot chocolate, we were back in business. Two weeks later, we counted up our profits: my share was three thousand dollars!

I invested my riches in the fertile fields of Wall Street, and in eighteen months, had turned my three thousand dollars into nearly one hundred thousand dollars. In fact, the Wall Street brokerage house was so impressed with my track record that the "big boys" invited me down to talk about how I picked my winners.

I arrived at the offices of the firm in lower Manhattan and told the receptionist I had an appointment with the manager. She gave me that "Uh-oh, here's trouble" look, largely, I think, because of my attire: I was still dressed in my policeman's uniform.

The meeting itself must have gone well, because at its conclusion the manager offered me a full-time job as a clerk, with the opportunity to begin studying immediately to become a broker. I was able to arrange a four-month leave from the police department as insurance to see if my new position worked out.

Did it ever! Using largely firm funds, plus my hundred thousand dollars, it took me less than one year to increase my net worth to more than one million dollars. In fact, nearly a million and a half. I was twenty-four years old, and became possibly the biggest jerk in New York City. In addition to the bachelor's pad, I had to have not one limousine but two (one in which to carry my friends around). I was out every night with the boys, chasing the girls and, all in all, going completely haywire.

Learning the Laws of Success

My girlfriend Maryanne, who is now my wife and president of Visible Changes, left me, saying that she liked me better when I was poor and to look her up if ever I reentered reality. I was indeed a long way from reality. In fact, one night, rather than pick up Maryanne in person for our date, I simply sent the limousine driver to fetch her. The driver returned, not with Maryanne, but with the following note: "If ever you decide to grow up, give me a call."

I considered that a license to party.

As my bankroll swelled, so did my head. I could do no wrong. The market was going one way—up—and I had the arrogance to think I was driving it. Wrong. I thought I was brilliant. Wrong again. And I thought it would never end. Oh, how wrong that was.

It took me less than a year to make more than a million dollars, and less than three months to lose it—plus $250,000 of borrowed money. The firm, one of the largest on Wall Street, went broke and closed its doors. I was worse than broke—I owed a quarter of a million dollars—and I was out of a job. My résumé read: high school graduate, cop, Christmas tree salesman, and failed Wall Street trader. Maryanne had left me, and once the limousines went, my friends went, too.

It was then that I did what a lot of other people with a lot of troubles often do: I went to the beach. Day after day, I'd look out over the water, thinking about what I was going to do with my life, but mainly worrying about the things I had already done wrong. It was here that I first met Abe, the aging industrialist who was to change—and probably save—my life.

"Sonny, sonny, the ship," said the old man who had sat down by my side. "It won't come in. There's a sandbar out there. You want the ship, go to the harbor." He spoke in broken English. "My name is Abe," he said.

I told him my name was John, and he asked, "Well, John, what do you see out there? Do you want to tell Abe something?"

Getting Naked

I said, "Yeah, I'll tell you something, Abe," and began to tell him about the police department and the Christmas trees and my rise and my fall and how my father said I'd never amount to anything and that I guessed he was right. At the end of my tale, I fully expected Abe to pat me on the shoulder and commiserate with me. He didn't.

"How old are you?" he asked.

I told him twenty-five.

"Twenty-five!!! You lucky son of a gun! You did it before you're forty. You're fifteen years ahead of me. Me, I lost my first million at forty. You lucky son of a gun." For the first time in weeks, I laughed.

We talked a while, and Abe said, "Well, what you think? You think you could beat me in a hundred-yard race?"

I looked at him and, again, I laughed. "Abe," I said, "I lost my money. Not my senses. You're three times my age."

He said, "Let's bet. I'll give you 10 to 1. Five hundred dollars if you beat me. You come here tomorrow morning."

What Abe didn't know was that I was in great shape. I worked out regularly at the gym, and when I was in officer's candidate school, I was graduated first out of 750 guys in the calisthenics and exercise drills, running up mountains with full packs and all that stuff. Today I might question whether I could beat him, but then I didn't. My only problem was that I didn't have fifty bucks, and I wasn't sure I could convince Maryanne (who had rejoined me after I became poor again) to loan me the money—even for a sure thing.

And so, when I went home that night, for the first time in weeks my head wasn't filled with self-hate and recriminations but rather with what this old man was up to. My mind was off my past and my problems, and I was looking forward to the future and the day of the race. No way that old man could beat me.

Maryanne was still skeptical, but she did give me the fifty

dollars, and I told her to prepare herself for the best candlelight dinner she'd eaten in months.

But I still couldn't figure out what Abe was up to. My only conclusion was that here's an old guy who feels sorry for me and wants to give me five hundred dollars. He knows the feeling of losing, and this is his way of doing a good deed. That had to be it.

The next day, as I approached the beach, for the first time I didn't look out at the water. I was a man with a mission, and that was to get this little exercise over with as quickly as possible and collect my five hundred dollars.

Over my shoulder, I heard his voice: "Did you mark the 100 yards?"

"No," I said, "I wanted to wait for you. I didn't want to cheat."

"So, what's the difference, 100, 105? So what? You think I'll die on an extra 5 yards? Mark it off. Don't worry about me."

After pacing off the 100 yards, I then noticed that Abe had a good-sized burlap bag slung over one shoulder. "Have you ever been to Aqueduct Racetrack?" he asked. I didn't like the tone of his voice.

"Yes, I have."

"And what happens when the one horsey comes out and looks good, and the next horsey comes out and he don't look too good? And they don't want everybody at the racetrack to bet on the horsey that looks good, so what do they do to that horsey so that the other horsey looks better?"

"Normally," I said, "they would put weights on him. Maybe twenty-five pounds or so, depending on how good the other horse is. It's called handicapping."

"Well," he said, "that's right. But me, I'm an old man. I can't carry weights with me, so I brought you this instead."

And he handed me the burlap bag, and told me to get into it. "Now what you think?"

Getting Naked

"I still think I can beat you."

And he said, "Funny you say that. I think you can, too. That's why you got to wear THIS."

That's when the blinkers came out and went on, and by this time, I was getting angry. It wasn't a game anymore. "What you think now?"

"I still think I can beat you."

"That's what I think. That's why you must run backwards." He didn't ask me what I thought.

"Do you think this is fair?" I asked.

"Okay. Then you can say, 'Go.' "

We took off. I ran a couple of steps, and, of course, fell down as he ran past the finish line. I took my blinders off, got out of the bag, and he returned. "Well, I beat you. Where's my money? What you think?" he asked.

"I think I just got hustled by a seventy-five-year-old man." And I took the fifty dollars and handed it to him.

"That's all you think? If that's all you learned from this, you're too stupid to ever become rich again. I don't want anything from you," he said, and threw the fifty dollars at me and started down the beach.

I ran after him and grabbed his arm. "Abe, Abe, you've got to understand. I'm only kidding you. I wanted to see if you were serious."

"You're about to see how serious. I'm very serious. You think I'd try to hustle you? You don't think I know what it feels like to lose everything you got? I also know that you don't learn nothing unless you pay for it."

"Okay, okay," I said.

"Did you learn that a seventy-five-year-old man can beat a twenty-five-year-old man at a race?"

"Yes," I said sheepishly.

"Now you tell me how I did that. But don't tell me now. You

tell me Monday morning [it was Friday], and if you don't have the right answer, you're not going to learn nothing else because you're too STUpid!"

I always paid my debts on my bets, even when it hurt, so I reached into my bathing suit pocket and handed over the fifty dollars. Feeling as stupid as he said I just might be, my main worry was how to tell Maryanne I had lost her fifty dollars. I felt shame, but I also felt curiosity. Who was this self-made millionaire (I later learned that Abe then had a net worth of more than $75 million, or in today's dollars, nearly $500 million), and what was he trying to teach me? And even more cryptically, WHY was he trying to teach it to me?

I left the beach that day with more questions than when I had arrived, but not once that day or over the entire weekend did I brood over the problems that had consumed me during the previous weeks. I had the premonition that I was in the presence of a very wise teacher. I spent the weekend with Maryanne (who, to this day, stands by me when I do dumb things), trying to figure out what Abe was trying to teach me.

Finally, on Monday morning, I went back to the beach. Abe was waiting for me.

"Well? What you think?"

And I said, "What I think you were trying to teach me, Abe, was that if you can set the rules to a game, then you can win the game."

"WELL!!!" he blurted out, "You, a high school graduate, can learn that, and my two sons, Ivy League graduates, those two characters in their fifties, are going to throw away my $75 million because they're too stupid to know these things."

And that's when he said, "We'll spend time together, and we'll sit down and go through it."

Over the next nine weeks, I met with Abe almost every day at the beach. He became my mentor, my teacher, my confidant, and my

Getting Naked

friend. He was the wisest man I've ever known in business or in life, and I never even knew his last name. Even though I begged him, he wouldn't tell it to me. In fact, Abe wanted to stop all contact with me at the end of our sessions. He knew what all wise teachers know—at a given point, the caterpillar is ready to become a butterfly and needs to fly off on its own.

Abe knew (and I now know) that if I could have made contact with him over these years, I'd always end up asking him the tough questions, rather than stumbling, falling down, making my own mistakes, and figuring out my own answers.

I did learn that Abe had turned over his empire and all but $5 million to his sons. His wife was dying of cancer, and her last wish was to go to the beach, so Abe had rented a condo for the summer season with a nurse in attendance. He was always at her side except for our beach sessions. He told me that he used time at the beach to think about his wife's health and what he would do with his life once she was gone.

At the end of our nine weeks together, Abe told me, "The thing I first noticed about you, John, was that you were so concentrated on your problem that you couldn't act. You were paralyzed, immobile. I had to break down your concentration. That was the whole idea behind the bet."

Abe knew what Vince Lombardi knew about comebacks. If Green Bay lost a game, Lombardi got the players through it by making the next week's practice such pure hell that they were too preoccupied to worry about the past. They were only thinking about how they could survive the week's practice.

But what was Lombardi really doing? He was diffusing their problem. Winners don't dwell on what they've lost. Maybe they lost because the other team was better. But when the Packers got back on the field the following Sunday, they were almost always better prepared than the other team, mentally and physically, and they'd almost always win. It can't be overemphasized: **Winners**

concentrate on the present and the future, not on the past.
That's what Abe taught me in those early days.

Now I'd like to complete the Abe story and pass along some of his philosophy that helped get my life back on track—and can get yours on track, too. Although we became friends, Abe was always a tough, no-nonsense codger. He began by asking me what every interviewer asks every interviewee at the beginning of every interview: What did I want to do with my life?

I told him I didn't know, but I thought I wanted to become a businessman. Abe then asked me how many businessmen I knew—"not many"—and what I knew about business—"not much."

Next, he brought out a yellow legal pad and asked, "Have you ever seen a balance sheet?"

I said, "Yes. Assets and liabilities." And he said, "Right. We're going to fill in YOU as a balance sheet."

On the liability side, I put down "Owes $250,000, no job, no trade."

He said, "Wait a minute, wait a minute. You started on the liability side. What does that mean to you?"

And I said, "I guess it means that I know my liabilities better than I know my assets."

He said, "That's exactly what it means, and anyone who knows his liabilities better than his assets is never gonna be a winner. He's gonna be a loser. Now put down your assets."

I wrote, "High school diploma."

He said, "If it was a college diploma I'd tell you from my own two sons to put it on the liability side." And then he said, "What else?"

I put down officer's candidate school and the police department academy. I said, "I'm not going to put down my Wall Street experience because I don't think it's an asset. That's it."

Getting Naked

He said, "Okay. Now let's look at your assets. And your liabilities. What you think of your balance sheet?"

And I said, "Not so great."

"Not so great?" he said. "It's terrible. It's a terrible balance sheet. How we gonna sell this to anyone? Look at this. Nothing. It stinks. Thank God," he said, "that you know nothing about how to fill out a balance sheet." And then he asked, "You speak English? Put that down as an asset. Do you know how many people out there don't even speak English? What are their chances of being successful? Put down 'Speak English.' "

"Can you read and write English? Put it down. That's an asset. Do you know currency?"

"Like how many yen there are to a dollar?"

"No, no, no, no. How many nickels, dimes, and quarters in a dollar, and how many combinations?"

And I said, "Of course."

"Put down, 'Know currency.' "

He said, "Do you have family?"

I said, "Yes."

"Put it down. They're an asset. Have you got friends?"

I said, "Not as many as I thought."

And he said, "But you got a few, right? Put it down. Do you know your way around the city? Can you get on the bus or train and get to New York? If somebody dropped you off in one of the five boroughs, could you figure out how to get to your home?"

"Yes."

"That's an asset," he said. "Do you know how many people can't do that? Put it down. Now," he said, "we've got to take the $250,000 off the liability side because anybody who had the rest of this balance sheet could never get a bank to loan him $250,000. That I can guarantee you. So, automatically, you're better off than someone with the same balance sheet because you already figured out how to get in debt for $250,000, and they can't do that." I began to feel better about myself.

"Now," he said, "how does this balance sheet rate with someone who graduates from Harvard or Yale?"

And I said, "Pretty bad."

"I agree," he said. "But are there any people who had a worse balance sheet than you when they started and went on to become millionaires?"

"Sure, there are a few."

"Not a few, sonny. Many, many men have had worse balance sheets than you and went on to become successful." And then Abe told me something that was to change my life: *"You must find these people and study under them. You must learn how they did what they did, and only then will you be ready to try it yourself."*

What Abe was telling me was that I could not apprentice under anyone with an Ivy League school diploma or an MBA, or someone who had come from the "right family" or had all the breaks in life. I would always feel inferior to those people, and they would always look down on me.

I needed, he said, to study under immigrants, people who had come to this country with nothing—no money, no English, no college, no connections, nothing—and had gone on to make great successes of themselves.

"Do you think somebody like me," asked Abe, "who didn't speak English, who didn't know how to read or write English, who didn't know currency, do you think that I could ever become a millionaire in this country? Of course I could. Three times. Do you think that I think I don't deserve to become a millionaire in this country? Of course I do. You and I, sonny, we have to take a different route. We have to work harder and, most of all, we have to believe in ourselves, because nobody else believes in us. That's where they're wrong, and we're right."

Getting Naked

On the last day of that summer season that I met with Abe, I begged, pleaded, and cajoled him to tell me his last name and phone number.

"I promise, Abe, I won't bug you. I just want to be able to get in touch with you, to hear how you're doing, and tell you how I'm doing."

"No, sonny," he said, "the apron strings must be cut." And then he told me about the wings and the nest.

He said, "You want to be a good parent, be sure there is a good nest where the children can feel safe and secure in, but you must teach them how to fly and tell them to leave the nest when it's time. Now is your time.

"John," he went on, "I've lost my entire fortune three times in my lifetime, and, late in life, I made another fortune and I turned it over to my children, and they're going to lose it. They will lose it because they didn't understand the game. What good is it if it's not looked at as a game?"

That's when I told him, "Abe, I've got it, I've got it. I'm ready to try it on my own."

He said, "You're not ready yet. You don't have the tools. How old do you want to be when you make it again?" And I picked forty because he said he was forty when he made it the first time.

"The whole idea is that you must know your time periods. If you set goals, they must be within time periods. If there aren't time periods, they aren't goals. You must study for the rest of your life, but for three years, you must study business under two or three successful men who began with nothing. Then you'll be ready to try it on your own."

"Abe, if this stuff works . . ."

He stopped me: "There are no 'ifs,' John; when you can implement what you learned, you'll make it. If you can't, you won't. Just learning it isn't good enough. It does not mean it doesn't work. Believe me, it works. 'If' should be deleted from your vocabulary. The word is 'when.' "

I said, "*When* I get it to work, I want to build a monument to you. I'll get permission from this town to build a statue of you here on this beach, and I'll donate the money."

He said, "No, John, no monument. When I look back over my life, the most fun that I had was the journey. I even enjoyed the failures, because I know how many times I've been tested and how many times I came back. It's like a piece of steel: You put it in the fire, and you take it out. You put it back, and it gets stronger. And it gets stronger. And it gets stronger.

"Now, looking back on my whole life, I'm happy because of the journey, and the fact that I made three fortunes is immaterial. It doesn't matter if I have a hundred million dollars or a billion, because at age seventy-five, I live 80 percent of my life in my dreams.

"What you can do for me," said Abe, "is *when* you make it— not *if*—*when* you make it, you share the knowledge I gave you this summer with other people. Teach others what I have taught you about business, about success, about living a good life."

I said, "Okay, that's a fair deal. I'll do that." And, in large measure, that's why I'm writing this book. It's for the "Old Man" on the beach. I'm honoring our contract.

Action Plan

● Create a personal balance sheet.

Be brutally honest with yourself—no one else has to see it—but concentrate on the positive side of your ledger. Rather than try to eliminate your weaknesses, we're going to concentrate on your strengths.

Getting Naked

- ### Don't be afraid of failure.

It's not an ugly word—except in school. We learn very little from
our successes. In fact, Thomas J. Watson, Sr., the founder of IBM,
once advised his protégés to "double your failure rate. Failure is
a teacher—a harsh one, perhaps, but the best. . . . So go ahead
and make mistakes. Make all you can. That's where you'll find
success—on the other side of failure." In Texas we say the true
test of a cowboy is not how many times he falls off his horse—but
how many times he gets back on.

- ### Focus on the present and the future.

Abe taught me that if I were too worried about a problem, I
couldn't solve it. Get rid of your guilt and other mental baggage.
Worrying causes doubt and doubt causes inaction. Don't let your
past, no matter what it entails, poison your future. We've all made
mistakes, and we've all got our messes to clean up. Abe knew that
my $250,000 debt was too overwhelming for me to deal with at
the time. I simply couldn't do anything about it. You, too, may
need to put some of your problems aside.

- ### To win the game, you must set the rules.

But before you set the rules, you must know the rules that are
already in play. To do this, you must study the ways and the means
by which other successful people became successful. In other
words, you must become a student of success, and then tailor what
you learn to who you are. Ultimately, the only rules that will work
for you are the ones that reflect your own personality and value
system. Two masters are worth listening to here. Ernest Heming-
way said that "to break the rules, you must first know the rules."
Once you know the rules, you can take the advice of the great
essayist Ralph Waldo Emerson: "When in doubt, trust thyself."

- ### Develop a "Lombardi mentality."

Lombardi understood that you don't "suit up" for the game unless
you expect to win, and that maxim applies to those who put on a

football uniform or a business suit. When Lombardi initially met his first professional football team as head coach, he told them that he had never been with a losing team and that they had never been a winning team, so they were going to do things his way. His way was the hard way, and that's the only way I know to *guarantee* success in any endeavor. There may be shorter routes to the top of the mountain, but my path—and the path I want you to get on in this book—is one step at a time, one foot after the other. It will get you there.

- **Success is both simple and difficult at the same time.**

The good news is that success and happiness grow out of mastering a very few fundamentals in life. The bad news is that we never totally master them. We only get closer to total mastery, so our pursuit is never ending. Richard Bach, who wrote *Jonathan Livingston Seagull,* has a simple test to determine whether your mission in life is accomplished: "If you're alive, it isn't."

- **Acquire a mentor.**

Abe was mine, but there are many others out there. Unfortunately, good mentor relationships cannot be forced or rushed. When the student is ready, the teacher will appear. In the meantime, if you're not studying under a mentor at this time, let me be yours through this book. You'd be honoring both Abe and me, and I'll do my best to live up to the responsibility.

Chapter 2

Washing Machines!

AFTER MY SUMMER with Abe, I went back to my friends on Wall Street and said, "Listen, I'm looking for a job—I don't care what kind of job it is—but it has to be working for a successful immigrant who didn't speak any English when he got started in America. Salary isn't important, nor are the number of hours I'll have to work."

The guys started laughing, probably thinking I had gotten too much sun during my visits to the beach.

My main objective for the next three years had nothing to do with making money. In fact, I can almost guarantee you that if your goal in life is to make money, it's almost certain that you never will. To achieve the pot of gold at the end of the rainbow, you have to concentrate on the rainbow, not on the gold. Only people who don't have money think they can get it by going directly for it. Those who have it know that money is a by-product of success. It is not success itself.

Most of us today want to start as high up the ladder in an organization as possible, taking the short route, or the fast track, to the top. Business school students gasp when I tell them the ideal entry-level position in business is at the bottom. The lower the better. If you learn a business from the bottom up, you'll always be much more comfortable and competent when you reach the top. You'll know your business better and, as important, you'll know your people better. At Visible Changes, neither Maryanne nor I ever asks a staff member to do a job that we haven't already done ourselves—or wouldn't do now.

Now I want to tell you two stories, one about an immigrant I'll call Bernie, who sold washing machines, and the other about a fellow I'll call Nick, who "rolls meatballs" for a living. Both are multimillionaires today. What I want you to take away from this chapter is a new appreciation for the words *commitment, drive,* and *determination.* If you've got these qualities, you can be at the bottom of the class in a lot of other areas and still become successful.

A Wall Street friend arranged for me to meet a fellow out on Long Island who had a company that was once successful but was now having difficulties. The man sold "industrial equipment," my friend said, and he really needed some help. Interest rates had gone so high that his customers couldn't get the financing to buy his products, and he was going under fast.

We set up an appointment.

I put on my best suit, borrowed Maryanne's car, and drove the seventeen miles from where I lived. Ironically, Bernie's factory and offices were only several blocks away from the beach I'd been going to each day. Grasping for anything, I considered this a good sign, an omen.

Until I reached his factory.

I walked through a set of double doors and found myself staring at a floor full of washing machines. "No way," I told myself. "I'm not doing this. Not from Wall Street to washing machines."

As I turned to leave, I heard a voice with a thick Yiddish accent from above: "Mr. McCormack, Mr. McCormack. We have an appointment. Where are you going?"

I said, "Sir, I just want to tell you it's been a pleasure meeting you, but I was misinformed. They told me you were in industrial equipment, not washing machines. I don't sell washing machines. Very nice meeting you." And, again, I headed for the door.

"Mr. McCormack, me, Bernie, I made $2 million two years ago selling these WASHING MACHINES!"

"Hmmm," I thought. "Well, what's a half hour. . . ."

Washing Machines!

Bernie, I soon learned, was just the man I was looking for. When he arrived in America after a sixteen-day sail from Germany, he had only a few dollars in his pocket and could not speak a word of English. Yiddish was the language of Bernie, my immigrant, soon-to-be friend.

When his ship finally entered New York Harbor, it was six o'clock in the morning of the craziest day of the year in New York City: St. Patrick's Day. Not only had Bernie never heard of St. Patrick's Day, he had never been drunk in his life; but somehow, by 8 A.M., he had found his way to a saloon in midtown Manhattan, and by 10 A.M., he was plowed.

"What a country!" thought Bernie. Beautiful women whom he didn't even know were hugging and kissing him, and a parade was forming outside—no doubt in his honor. Big, burly Irishmen were slapping him on the back and buying him mug after mug of beer. The more he drank, the happier he got, and the happier he got, the more he drank.

"It was the greatest day of my life," Bernie recalls.

Bernie began his new life in a little apartment in the Lower Manhattan area of New York City. Every day, he would walk to a diner near his home for lunch and order the same meal from the same waitress: ham and eggs. He couldn't read the menu, so he simply said those three words.

One day, however, a fellow diner sat down on the stool next to him, and Bernie listened intently to the man's order. "Ham and *cheese*," the man said, and soon afterward, a heaping sandwich of ham and hot melted cheese appeared. Bernie was awed, and excited.

The following day, the waitress approached him and said, "I know, I know, 'Ham and eggs,' " and Bernie smiled, shook his head, and said, "No, ham and *cheese*."

The waitress smiled, stepped back, and said, "White or rye?"

"Ham and *eggs*," Bernie replied.

It wasn't easy for Bernie in the beginning, just as it wasn't easy for the millions of immigrants who came before him, but they brought with them both a dream for a new life and, most important, the drive to turn their dream into reality. If you're not willing to do "whatever it takes" to become successful, then, I guarantee you, you never will become successful.

Here's what it took for Bernie:

Soon after arriving in America, Bernie joined the U.S. Navy, partly for regular meals and partly for a regular paycheck.

Because he had had a smattering of electrical training in Europe, he was placed in the radar unit aboard an aircraft carrier that soon found itself at sea for twenty-one days of maneuvers off the Atlantic Coast.

Several days into the exercises, something happened that sounds as though it would be a minor problem onshore, but in fact is a major one at sea: the washing machines broke down. Sheets and clothes, which began to collect in small piles, soon became great heaps and then grew into mountains. Sailors began to smell, and tempers began to foul. Dragging the laundry over the side of the ship through salt water did no good at all.

Exasperated, the admiral in charge decided to scrap the mission and return to port. Bernie, who had heard about the problem through a Yiddish-speaking friend, asked for a chance to repair the machines. The task was easy, and Bernie thought nothing of it.

The admiral, however, was so delighted that he wanted to meet the man who had saved his maneuvers, and Bernie was summoned to quarters—without a translator.

Bernie later told me, "As a foreigner who doesn't speak English in the navy, you soon learn that you do better with the yesses than with the noes, so I started 'yessing' the admiral."

Washing Machines!

"You seem to know electronics very well," the admiral said.

"Yes, sir."

"We never looked at this as a serious problem, but obviously if you can't keep things clean on a ship, including laundry, you can't carry on."

"Yes, sir."

"So what I'm thinking of doing is setting up a special department in New Jersey where all they will do is work on laundry equipment for our ships. Would you be interested?"

"Yes, sir."

"We'll send you to school, and then if there's a problem aboard a ship off the coast, we'll helicopter you out and you can troubleshoot for us."

"Yes, sir."

"Okay. We'll do it right away."

"Yes, sir."

That very afternoon, Bernie was carted off the carrier aboard a helicopter en route for laundry repair school in New Jersey. It seems the navy had problems with all of its washers and dryers, and it had a lot of washers and dryers: aboard ships, at military bases, in officers' homes, and so on, and eventually Bernie was put in charge of fixing all of them.

One day, he received a telephone call that a navy ship had collided with a private vessel in New York Harbor, and the navy needed him to assess the damage to the laundry facilities of both. Bernie boarded a helicopter and set about his duties.

When he boarded the private ship and was escorted to the laundry room, he recalls (and his eyes light up, even to this day), "You wouldn't believe these washing machines. Stainless steel inside, and tubs that went around. The Rolls Royce of washing machines!"

A dream began to form.

Learning the Laws of Success

After finishing his tour of duty, Bernie wrote the chairman of the manufacturing company in Europe, telling him he'd like to represent his line of washing machines in America. He knew he could sell them.

The chairman wrote back promptly, explaining that negotiations were already well under way with a number of large U.S. distributors. "I'll keep you in mind, but don't hold your breath," was the way Bernie interpreted the letter.

Now, pay attention here, because what Bernie did next is what sets him apart from 99.9 percent of the rest of us: He took his life savings, which amounted to less than five hundred dollars, and bought a round-trip ticket and one new business suit. He left LaGuardia Airport in New York, bound for Sweden, with his suit on his back, a duffel bag with a clean shirt and shaving gear in his hand, and only a few dollars in his pocket. Bernie was about to take his shot.

His wife stayed home and prayed.

Upon arrival, Bernie met with the chairman of the board, who was friendly but to the point: "How much money do you have to get this distributorship going?"

Bernie had none but was sure that if he could get the machines on credit, he could sell them and then pay the manufacturer.

"Thanks for stopping by," said the chairman.

That night Bernie slept in miserable quarters without even a shower but, nevertheless, showed up at the chairman's office the next day without an appointment. He explained, "I forgot to tell you yesterday a few things about how I intend to get your machinery into different locations." Bernie then related his plan to buy a station wagon, cut off its back, wedge in a washing machine, and then drive on sales calls, door to door, laundromat to laundromat. He had already taken the measurements, and the machine would fit perfectly.

"We'll let you know," said the chairman.

Washing Machines!

The next day Bernie was back at the chairman's door, looking and feeling, in his own words, "rumpled, wrinkled, ashamed, and totally desperate."

"This is a matter of life and death," he began. "This is the most important thing in my life to me and my wife. I know your machinery is good; I know its quality; I know I can sell it; I need a chance."

Finally the chairman relented, betting on Bernie's persistence rather than his bankbook, and decided to give him a shot. It turned out to be a good bet.

As you can imagine, Bernie prospered. He did what he had promised and cut out the back of the station wagon, and started down Delancey Street, hauling his marvelous washing machine from laundromat to laundromat. He immersed himself in his sales. He knew his machines were better: they used one-third the soap and got three times the suds, and, more important, they rinsed the soap totally out of the clothes. Bernie became the educator, preaching his clean-clothes catechism not only to his customers but to his customers' customers. He'd spend his days at the laundromats, explaining the virtues of his machines to anyone he could collar. He believed in an educated consumer, and he was right.

Soon Bernie's machines became so busy, and the competitors' so idle, that the managers started telling the owners they needed more.

"I finally began to get somewhere," recalls Bernie. The problem was that while he was doing well in a several-block area of Manhattan, Bernie was virtually unknown in the wider circle of the washing machine world, the big time where an institution might buy, say, fifty or a hundred machines at a time.

And there was another problem: "Nobody big," he said, "wanted to do business with me. I was a nobody."

But this nobody had the foresight to recognize his shortcomings and hire a somebody. That somebody was one of the top salesmen in the industry, and he knew every other "somebody" in the business.

Bernie hired his recruit for twice his previous salary and ten times what he himself was making, and soon Bernie's world was no longer Delancey Street. It was the entire United States of America! Trade shows. Conventions. Sales calls. High-volume distributors.

"You don't know how many times my family had hot dogs for dinner—sometimes four nights a week—and then I'd think about those paychecks I was writing. He was worth it, but I couldn't afford it. Sometimes I cried over it, because I really thought I was giving my family the shaft, but I thought it was our only shot. I had to keep going."

On the day I first met Bernie, he was in the middle of another crisis. His sales had dropped from more than $10 million to less than $5 million in twenty-four months. He had five warehouses full of equipment and a tugboat in New York Harbor with more of the same. Interest rates were so high and money so scarce that Bernie's customers could no longer afford his machines. His distributors were drying up or drifting away.

Worse, he was preparing to deliver a major speech to the largest distributors in the country at their annual get-together in Las Vegas, and he wanted my opinion. The theme of the speech was how he was going to sell all of these stockpiled washing machines.

I read it and decided to give it to him straight: "That's it?" I asked. "You can't be serious."

He hired me on the spot as a consultant. My first assignment?

"You're so smart, Mr. McCormack, you do the speech."

A week later, I walked into his office and announced, "I've got it."

Washing Machines!

"Wait here," he said. A few minutes later, Bernie returned and announced that rather than read the speech to him, I was to deliver it to his entire organization, which he had just assembled in his conference room.

Bernie had rounded up every warm body he could find, including secretaries and salesmen, the loading dock crew and the sales manager. An audience of about eighty.

Bernie got things started: "I'd like to introduce you to Mr. McCormack. He's going to give this speech in Las Vegas to save our company and all our jobs. With no further ado, Mr. McCormack, get up here."

Now, I had done some public speaking before, and in fact had won the title for best public speaker in officer's candidate school, but I really wasn't prepared for this. I decided to give it to them straight:

"I've looked at all your information and data, and I must tell you, I'm very impressed with your company. Your machinery is clearly the best in the marketplace, and that is a compliment to each and every one of you in this room. However, you need to know that producing the best machinery and being able to sell the best machinery are two very different things.

"Obviously, if your sales have dropped in half in twenty-four months—and I hope everybody knows this—you are in deep trouble as a company.

"Why should we kid each other?" I asked them. "We're family here, and we're all dependent on each other. Now, the situation, as I see it, is that you have five warehouses full of equipment with more of it parked on a boat out in the harbor.

"So not only are you paying for inventory and paying interest on it, now you've got to pay for the storage of this inventory, plus you're slowing down the factory over there. They're down to a four-day workweek.

"The problem isn't with you or your equipment. It's with the banking system. Interest rates are now at 15 percent, and the banks don't believe that the people who buy your machines can afford to pay that rate. Bernie here thinks they can.

"So," I said, "what's the difference if we go broke with these machines sitting here in the warehouses or if we go broke putting our equipment into the stores, and we collect from the buyers a monthly payment? In effect, we will become the bank."

During the previous week, I had worked out a plan in which our distributors would sell the machinery on time and would get paid their 40 percent when the monthly payments came in. We'd get the remaining 60 percent. We'd eliminate our inventory problem and create a stream of cash to start paying our bills.

My credibility, I think, came from my Wall Street experience. The workers were, probably for the first time in a long time, excited about their prospects.

Bernie wasn't so sure, but he reluctantly agreed to let me take the road show to Las Vegas and try it in the big time: the national distributors' meeting.

The distributors treated me like some great guru, a savior with financing secrets that would change the industry. I explained to them that once we developed a track record of receiving our monthly payments, the banks would be only too happy to get back in the lending business to our customers. We simply needed a stopgap remedy to build that track record. In the meantime, things wouldn't be so bad.

The distributors would get 40 percent of the payment money, plus the 18 percent interest attached to each payment. What was wrong with that?

They loved the idea. They were back in business, and couldn't wait to get back on the street. But if they were delighted, Bernie was ecstatic. He wanted me to extend my trip, taking a swing

Washing Machines!

through southern California, northern California, Washington, and back to Las Vegas. We'll just change your airline ticket, he said. No problem.

Thus I began my career as a washing machine salesman, and, I must confess, I enjoyed it. I was getting a little bit of recognition, and all of the distributors wanted to meet with me, the new kid on the block, rather than with Bernie or anyone else.

Things began to pop. I walked into a laundromat in California with the distributor, and the owner started grilling me about washing machine cycles, etc. "Let me tell you something," I told him. "I have nothing to do with the inner workings of the machine itself. If you want that, we have an 800 number, and the technical guys will answer all your questions.

"Now your question to me should not be, 'Does this $9,000 piece of machinery cycle three hundred times?' When you buy an automobile, do you ask how many times the cylinders go up and down in a minute? Who cares? The question is, 'Does the machine do what it's supposed to do?' Well, I'm here to tell you that no machine on the market can match ours, and I can prove it to you.

"Do the clothes get clean? How many pounds can we put in it? How many loads can it turn in an hour? We can figure out some cash flows for you." And on and on.

The guy stopped me: "It's obvious," he said, "that we need this piece of equipment in here immediately. Can you get it here tomorrow?"

The distributor was floored: "I've spent the last year trying to sell this man," he said. "He always asks me all these questions, and you tell him to forget the questions or call the factory, and the next thing I know you're talking to him about things I've never heard about before. And the guy buys the machine!"

To me, it was easy. Remember Abe? *"He who makes the rules . . ."*

Learning the Laws of Success

Then things really began to move. I soon learned that the best time to approach a laundromat owner is between 6 P.M. and 10 P.M. They're always in the shop then, cleaning up, preparing for the next day. So I'd waltz in, start up a conversation, and waltz out with the orders. In one week, I sold more than a hundred of Bernie's marvelous washing machines. What I didn't know at the time was that I was still playing in the minor leagues. The majors take place in Michigan, the washing machine capital of the country.

Michigan combines a number of qualities that make it perfect for the laundromat business. First, it's mainly a blue-collar state, and blue-collar workers generally come home dirty and with dirty clothes. And second, because of the heavy industry in the area, the water is extremely hard, which translates into no soap suds unless an expensive water softener is added to the washing machine. Consequently, most families get their clothes cleaned at the local laundromat.

It was here in Ann Arbor that I first met Big Jim, who was to become one of my heroes. Big Jim, who was one of our biggest distributors, by all accounts didn't stand a chance in life. Born into poverty, his parents died when he was just an infant. At age five or six, he hung around the neighborhood tavern, shining shoes for nickels. Today he is a millionaire with about thirty "supergiant" laundromats in the Ann Arbor area. These are huge stores—5,000 to 8,000 square feet—with 150 to 250 pieces of equipment.

I stayed at Big Jim's home for three days, and he told me tales of how he just kept putting his nickels and dimes together to build his business. He began in the bar business—something I've always wanted to do—but his employees were stealing him blind, so he got into the jukebox racket, before Bernie convinced him that washing machines were more profitable than jukeboxes.

Washing Machines!

He began as a distributor but became intrigued with the hard-water problem in the area, so he decided to take his shot: a long shot. He located a cluster of apartments and decided to build an eight-thousand-square-foot facility. It was a happening. It even had a bar in it.

The concept took off, and as soon as Big Jim recouped his investment, he dumped his money into a second megacenter. And then another one. To hear him tell it, "Before I knew it, I had thirty stores, and I was a rich man."

With Big Jim's help, I sold more than a million dollars' worth of washing machines during my short visit. Things were humming for me and buzzing for Bernie. His factory was working twenty-four hours a day, and we didn't even need a warehouse: the machines were being shipped as fast as he could turn them out. In just eighteen months we had tripled his sales, and there was no ceiling in sight.

Bernie went on to become so powerful in the industry that he could literally write his own ticket. He bought a dry-cleaning company, a dryer company, and a huge washing machine manufacturing company in Texas.

But don't make the mistake of thinking that anything ever came easy for Bernie. There is a poem that includes the lines, "Johnny Nolan has a patch on his rear. / Kids chase him. . . ."

Sure, Bernie knew he had patches on his pants and, of course he was embarrassed, but he knew he still had to make his sales calls. That was more important than the patches. Bernie taught me that all of us have patches of one sort or another, but if we continue to "make the calls," we can overcome any handicaps or shortcomings.

To this day, I can recall my embarrassment when as a child I was teased by the neighborhood kids because of my shiny pants. Each September, before school started, my mother would buy me a new pair of blue trousers, and they had to last the entire year. When they got wrinkled, she'd press them, and by March or April, I was a virtual reflector walking down the block. Those memories, I'm afraid, stay with us forever.

After a year and a half with Bernie, it was about time to move on. Bernie asked me to stay, and in fact offered me a shot at the presidency of his company and a big bonus. After Abe, however, I had forever forsaken short-term thinking and decision making, and I had no difficulty in turning my good friend down.

I had my own dreams to pursue, and I was in search of another mentor to complete the thirty-six-month program I had set out with Abe.

Action Plan

- **Do whatever it takes.**

Forget what others may think. Forget about the "patches on your pants," whatever they may be. Forget what your friends might think about your driving an old clunker, rather than a BMW you bought on time because you couldn't afford it. Be prepared to make all of the sacrifices necessary to become a success. Your efforts today will pay off in multiples tomorrow.

- **Hard work works, and winners work hard.**

There simply is no substitute for putting in the hours. While "working smarter, not harder" has lately come into vogue, a better formula is to work smarter, faster, *and* harder. Accept it as one of McCormack's Commandments that it is better to work a hundred hours for yourself than forty for someone else.

- **Act decisively.**

Make your decisions as they come with the best information you have. It is easier in most cases to make a corrective action later

Washing Machines!

than it is to recapture an opportunity lost through inaction or indecision. When Bernie saw an opportunity to represent the "Rolls Royce of washing machines" in America, he didn't dawdle. He bought the ticket. Norman Vincent Peale writes, "If you put off everything till you're sure of it, you'll get nothing done." Put another way, we all know what happens to people who stay in the middle of the road: they get run over.

- **Don't look down on any industry.**

Millionaires come from all walks of life, not just the "glamorous professions," such as banking, investing, and mergers and acquisitions. Go into businesses that are not considered businesses. Some of my best friends have made millions in garbage pickup, junk-yards, funeral homes, and, yes, cutting hair.

- **Don't look down on any location.**

You don't need to eat, drink, and breathe New York in order to become successful. In fact, New York is a terrible place for entrepreneurs: the rents are too high, the competition is too great, and the values are all messed up. Pick a location where you'd like to live, where you'd like to raise your children, and where the resources exist to support your business. Nine times out of ten, New York won't even make the short list.

- **If you don't have it, hire it.**

You cannot be expert in all things, and one of the wisest insights an entrepreneur can have is to realize his or her own limitations. Bernie hired a man for a salary he couldn't afford, and it transformed his business. Years later, when he hired me, he had the foresight to bring someone in from outside his industry because he realized he was stumped: he knew that the credit crunch was killing his business, but he didn't know how to solve it. He had a financial problem, not a washing machine problem, so he brought in a financial person to help him solve it. For him it was impossible. For me, it was easy.

- ## There's nothing wrong with starting poor, and there's no need to affect being rich.

Big Jim taught me two important lessons: first, great wealth can come from any denomination—his came from nickels, dimes, and quarters—and second, once you get an idea that works, multiply it out. Once he became successful with one laundromat, he put in a second, and a third, and so on. It was a business he knew from the inside out, so he stuck with it. We've done the same with Visible Changes. We can make a couple hundred thousand dollars a year with every additional salon we open.

- ## Do not go outside of the business you know best.

It was Uncle Sam's tax code (which, in the early eighties, was 70 percent for someone in my bracket) that enticed me into the real estate business. Even if I had made money, as I had intended to do, the "lost opportunity" costs still would have been horrible. If I had stayed closer to home and spent that time expanding Visible Changes, I would have been much better off.

- ## Get focused.

Once you've determined what you want to do, lock it in your mind and discard any activities that don't contribute to your goal. Although it was painful, Bernie had to disregard even the food he was putting on his family table when he was building his business. Reaching that goal had to override all other considerations. When you're just starting out, choose your goal, commit to it, and don't turn back. A wonderful poem by W. H. Murray, "Until One Is Committed," sums it up:

Washing Machines!

Until one is committed

There is hesitancy, the chance to draw back,
Always ineffectiveness.
Concerning all acts of initiative (and creation),
There is one elementary truth,
The ignorance of which kills countless ideas
And splendid plans:
That the moment one definitely commits oneself,
Then Providence moves too.
All sorts of things occur to help one
That would never otherwise have occurred.
A whole stream of events issues from the decision,
Raising in one's favor all manner
Of unforeseen incidents and meetings
And material assistance,
Which no man could have dreamt
Would have come his way.

I have learned a deep respect
For one of Goethe's couplets:

"Whatever you can do, or dream you can, *begin it.*
Boldness has *genius, power,* and *magic* in it."

Chapter 3

Meatballs for Millions

$\mathbf{A}$T THE END of my tenure with Bernie, Nick, the catering king, entered my life. This was another example of the teacher appearing at precisely the moment the student is ready for the lesson.

I met Nick soon after making a sales call at his catering hall. I was trying to sell him a couple of Bernie's machines. Nick told me I was too smart to be selling washing machines. I told him about Abe and how I had vowed to study for three years under successful immigrants who had come to this country with nothing. Nick, who was to become my next mentor, fit that description perfectly.

Born and raised in war-torn Italy, Nick was one of ten children in a dirt-poor family that struggled to survive during the hated Mussolini regime. Nick would later tell me that we in America really don't know suffering because we don't know the pain of hunger.

The family was so impoverished that the boys in the family would eat pasta for four days and fast for the fifth. There simply wasn't enough food to go around. Nick's childhood toys were potatoes, which his mother let him play with before she'd cook them. He would mentally transform his potatoes into locomotives and automobiles and other imaginings of a child. To this day, he will tell you they were terrific toys.

Following the war, Nick's parents realized that there was no future for their children in ravaged Italy, so they made a difficult decision. After each boy turned sixteen, he was taken to the wharf and put on board a ship to find a new life in America.

Nick didn't make his trip, however, until he was twenty. At sixteen he was seriously ill. By the time he recovered, the army grabbed him for two years. When he finally left his homeland, he did so as a merchant marine, having secured a position as a "stoker" on a ship bound for America. Nick's chief duty was to shovel coal into the furnace to generate the power to keep the ship moving.

What Nick didn't know at the time was that there were two Americas—North America and South America—and the ship he had signed on was destined for the wrong one. "I'd look for the big buildings," he says, "and I couldn't find them." And then it was back and forth to Europe for nearly three years before he was able to transfer to a ship heading for North America. Only this time, it was destined for Canada.

Outside of Philadelphia, Nick's luck changed. The ship's main engine broke down, and the vessel limped into port for repair. Nick went up to the deck and discovered what he had been looking for for years: tall buildings!

Nick was off like a shot, down to his locker, where he put on two shirts, three pair of underwear, and then his pants.

He went back up on deck and jumped overboard into the icy January waters. He was a poor swimmer and nearly froze to death before he floundered to shore.

Dripping wet, speaking not a word of English, and without a penny in his pocket, Nick shivered off through the streets of Philadelphia to find his new life. He finally ran into a Spanish fellow who spoke broken Italian, and asked him for directions to New York. The man was a Samaritan.

He took Nick in, dried off his clothes, and told him to go to Brooklyn, because that was where all the Italians in New York lived. He took Nick to the train station and bought him a ticket. Nick was on his way.

According to Abe's theory, I had found myself the perfect mentor: When he arrived in America, he was broke, he didn't

Meatballs for Millions

know the currency, he couldn't speak a word of our language, and he couldn't find his way around the city. In fact, for years he couldn't even find the country! If this guy could become a millionaire many times over, certainly I stood a chance.

In Brooklyn Nick found enclaves of Italians, including some from his homeland village, who, of course, had known of his family for years. They took him in, and within three days, Nick had applied for a job as a dishwasher in an Italian restaurant. The general manager, also an Italian, took a liking to Nick and decided to give him a chance. Nick had become a fledgling participant in the American dream.

Shrewdly Nick made plans to meet the owner of the restaurant. He wanted to assure the owner that he would do a good job and would take seriously any new responsibilities. He also thought that if he could meet the owner, he would better his chances for future advancement. Here's what he did:

Nick went into the bathroom, scrubbed it down with the scrubber, and then took a toothbrush and cleaned between every tile. The bathroom was spotless, and the results were almost instantaneous. Nick called this work his "calling card."

"Have you seen the john?" asked the owner. "Who's new on staff?"

Moments later, Nick was face to face with the owner.

A week later when the salad man quit, Nick got the job. He soon learned that 25 percent of the salads were being thrown out because by the end of the night they hadn't been sold, and by the next morning the lettuce leaves had turned brown.

When Nick told his neighbor, an old Italian woman, about his good fortune ("I'm the new salad man"), he remarked about the wastefulness in America and the problem with the lettuce leaves. She told Nick that all he had to do was rinse the leaves in a solution of baking soda and water, and they would stay fresh, white, and healthy. As of the next day, Nick started doing this on his own and putting them out for sale.

It was the bookkeeper who first got suspicious: "What's going on with the salads?" he asked the owner. "The salad bill has been cut by 25 per cent. You must be putting out smaller or cheaper salads. You'd better jump on it."

So the owner asked Nick, "What are you doing? Let me see the salads." They looked okay, and that's when Nick showed him his trick. He was soon off to chef's school, at the owner's expense, where again he excelled.

Eventually Nick found his way to a catering job in Queens and started buying up storefront property with little apartments above them. They all cost the same, $20,000, and they could be had for a down payment of $2,000. Nick and his wife lived upstairs in one of these tiny units and rented out the downstairs to pay the notes. In a small way, he had entered the real estate business.

Then he saw what appeared to him as an opportunity. A Jewish catering hall on Queens Boulevard was on the market. It had an upstairs and a downstairs, was sixty feet wide and a hundred feet deep, and was sandwiched between a gas station on the left side and a car wash on the right. To Nick it was beautiful. To anyone else, it was pitiful. The asking price was $175,000 in 1968, but a $20,000 down payment would get him into the business. Nick went back to his real estate agent and told him to sell everything. He needed the cash to buy his own business.

His first soiree was a kosher Jewish wedding, and he didn't make a dime. He thought he could trim costs and make a profit if he could convince his Jewish clientele to accept certain changes in the methods of preparing the food. He took prospective clients on tours of his kitchen to emphasize its cleanliness. The first year he did $175,000 in sales, for a net profit of zero.

Nick, his wife, and their two small children were living on seventy-five dollars a week. Nick was depressed and scared.

Meatballs for Millions

On some nights, Nick will tell you today, he would cry on his way home on the bus and the train: His family was suffering, and he was failing. He felt powerless. He had gambled everything, and he had lost. Failure was imminent and unavoidable.

At the end of eighteen months of this misery, Nick finally concluded that even with all of his improvements—better food, cleaner facilities, better service—he still couldn't make a profit. He was always behind.

In desperation, he turned to his suppliers for advice. What was he doing wrong? To them, it was apparent: "Your place is a dump. Only people with no money would think of coming here. You've got only fourteen parking spaces, not to mention the car wash and the gas station on each side of your establishment."

Nick visited his competitors and realized his suppliers were right. His place was a dump in comparison. But the little Italian runaway decided to fight one more time. Like Bernie, he had no past to go back to, so forward was the only way.

He went down to a local art supply store and asked if they knew a starving artist who might be able to draw a man's dreams in exchange for some food. They did, and Nick commissioned him to draw the most beautiful catering restaurant he could imagine. Nick then placed the renderings around his lobby and invited his suppliers back.

"I'm going to take your advice," he told them. "You're right, my place is a dump, but I'm going to make it beautiful. This is what it is going to look like," he said, showing off his drawings. "The banks," he told them, "don't know Nick, and won't lend me money. But I've worked with you here and in my previous job for the past ten years, and you know I'm an honest man."

Nick convinced each of them to loan him $25,000 in exchange for exclusive five-year contracts on his supplies. Each year, for five years, Nick told them, he would repay 20 percent of their loan plus 20 percent interest. Oh, one other thing. He wanted them to provide all supplies to him for the first year and spread the billing over the next five years.

Every one of them bought the deal. Talk about innovative financing!!! Nick calls it "Italian math."

Nick then hired an architect and told him he could give him five thousand dollars up front and the remainder in two years, plus interest, of course. The architect went for it.

Then Nick got another brainstorm. Since most New Yorkers plan their weddings far in advance, why not sell them on what his place would look like when the renovation was complete? Again, out came the drawings, and this time Nick was ready to offer a deal:

"In the old place," he told his clients, "I'd charge you $12 per head to cater your wedding. The price goes up to $25 in the new place, which your lovely daughter no doubt deserves. If you'll just bear with me until I finish my renovation—here, let me show you my drawings—I'll give you the deal of your life. The new place at the old price. *But only if you pay me in advance.*"

After he sold about five or six of these packages, he increased his prices to $40 later or $20 if you pay now, and he soon had $175,000 in cash in hand. The budget for his remodeling, however, had gotten as large as his dream. The estimated cost had risen to $650,000, and he thought he could come up with no more than $300,000.

That's where family came in. Nick's brothers were general contractors and tradesmen, and Nick told them they needed to convince their subcontractors to do the work and take 25 percent up front and the remainder on a five-year payout. Again, the family name and reputation were magic.

The renovation of the outside and the gutting of the inside began in earnest. Nick told the subcontractors he needed a nine-month project completed in three because he couldn't afford to be

Meatballs for Millions

shut down for so long without a cash flow. The brothers themselves worked nearly round the clock to meet the three-month deadline and oversee the overall operations.

The project became a mission, and the mission was completed, on time. Only hours away from opening night (a lavish wedding reception), a small cloud appeared on Nick's horizon. He had forgotten to apply for his new operating permit, and no permit meant no business. Without exception. Well, actually with *one* exception, and that was a $500 bribe to the building inspector, whom Nick paid and invited in for some of the wedding cake.

Like all good wedding stories, the bride and the bridegroom as well as the caterers, the construction workers, the suppliers, the building inspector, and, yes, Nick and his family, lived happily ever after.

Indeed, the reputation of Nick's catering service soared, as did his sales. The year before his remodeling, he did $175,000 in sales with no profit. The year after, sales rose to $800,000 with a 50 percent profit. The following year sales increased to $1.2 million with a 55 percent profit, and Nick paid off all his creditors. Nick was well on his way to becoming the multimillionaire he is today.

At one point Nick asked me, "John, do you think anyone would ever pay me a million dollars a year to roll meatballs? Of course not. That's why I had to start my own business, so I could pay a million dollars to myself. Nobody else would bet on me, so I had to bet on me."

I'll close this chapter with one more Nick story that taught me a lot about both friendship and business. We got together on a real estate deal in Greenwich, Connecticut, that involved buying fifty-three condominium apartments that we planned to redo and sell for a handsome profit. The banks loaned us only $11 million, but before we were through, it looked as if the cost would be close to $20 million. The construction expenses were going through the roof, and our money appeared to be going down a bottomless rat-hole.

I was getting cash calls of $400,000 a week with no end in sight. I figured I'd better go to Connecticut to sort things out. I told Maryanne I'd be gone three days—and returned sixty-three days later. After that, I went back every other week for a year and a half. It was a nightmare: Theft. Kickbacks. The whole nine yards.

"Nick," I said, "I can't afford to put up any more cash. This could kill Visible Changes. I'm almost out of money." I wanted to walk the deal, but Nick said, "No, John, once you commit, you've got to stay in whether you win or you lose. You gave your word."

What Nick did was commit to funding the cash calls, and soon he had about $5 million more in the deal than I did—and he refused to dilute my percentage of ownership. He told me just to keep on working as hard as I could to make it work.

On one trip to the building site, I arrived at LaGuardia Airport, looking haggard, hassled, and tired. I had spent three hours on the plane furiously reading contracts, grinding numbers, making contingency plans, and, frankly, freaking out.

Nick met me at the gate, calm as could be, in his thousand-dollar custom-made Italian suit, looking tan, fit, and never better. As we got into his car, he slipped a cassette of his favorite opera music into the player, and we took off for Connecticut with him humming and my head buzzing.

I looked over at Nick, and then I looked at myself in the visor mirror.

"Nick," I said, "I don't understand it. You don't seem to be worried about a thing, you look great, and I'm a wreck. What's the deal?"

And that's when he told me about Italians and their bankers.

"John," he began, "in Italy there are two kinds of people: bankers and those who want to borrow from bankers.

Meatballs for Millions

"Further, there are two types of bankers: One type lends money on good land value, so he might lend you 50 percent of the value on a good piece of property. This banker sleeps real good when he puts his head on his pillow. Now, the man who borrowed the money doesn't sleep too good because he wants to make sure the banker gets paid off so he can keep his good property.

"The other type of banker is a little lazy, and he doesn't even look at the property. He loans 125 percent of its value. Then he realizes he shouldn't have been so lazy. Now, at night this banker doesn't sleep good at all. But the man who borrowed the money sleeps like a rock, because he's not really worried about how he's going to pay back that money.

"Now, John, we've got our situation. We get involved in this project, and the project doesn't go too well, and I watch you and you watch me, and we are interested in each other's problems as well as our own. Now I like that about you, John. You don't say, 'Hey, Nick, you're not doing your job.' You just keep working, and you are doing a good job at the work.

"Now, when the money calls come, and you don't have any more money, I say, 'But Johnny is doing all of the work, so I think I should put up the money. So I put up a little more money than you, and you put up a little more work than me—but John, that isn't why I can go up to Connecticut and look so good and sleep so good; and honestly, I look over at you, and you look terrible.

"I feel sorry for you because you don't deserve to look terrible, because you've been a very smart boy, but I know from my banking experience that *no two people should ever worry about the same problem.*

"Now we have our situation again, a $20 million project, and that is a lot of money to two people, but if this project doesn't work out, God forbid, John McCormack might have to declare bankruptcy—I think they call it that. Nick will be hurt a bit, but it won't have to be bankruptcy. If the project does work out, it is going to work out because someone worried about it and made sure that it did work out.

"Now, John, I look at it this way: The worst thing that can happen to me if the project doesn't work out is called a 'tax write-off.' That's what I have—a big tax write-off or a little tax write-off, depending on how well you do at figuring out our problem and sleeping at night. The reason I look so good is because when I see you look so bad, I know that the problem is going to be fixed."

After I finished calling him a number of names, I realized he was right. I had entered into a deal with someone who could much better afford to be in it than I could. I was luckier than most. If we needed more cash, I knew Nick could come up with it. All I had to do was figure out the problems. I must say, though, our relationship was severely tested—and ultimately strengthened—during this period. I don't have the words to tell you the importance to me of our relationship. Nick will always be my mentor—and my friend.

Action Plan

- **Start at the bottom.**

There is no substitute for working your way up and learning every aspect of the business every step of the way. Remember Nick and his toothbrush? Confidence comes much more from experience than it does from knowledge or theory, and the return on investment for time spent at the lower rungs of the ladder will always pay off at the top.

- **Discipline, discipline, discipline.**

Simply put, no one I've ever known—from athletes to businesspeople—who is successful ever got that way without a strict

Meatballs for Millions

regimen of self-discipline. You must train yourself to do the things you don't want to do—*when you don't want to do them.*

● Good timing.

In business, as well as in romance, timing is critical to getting the job done. You've got to be in the right place at the right time and be prepared to act. Perhaps William Shakespeare said it best:

> There is a tide in the affairs of men,
> Which, taken at the flood, leads on to fortune;
> Omitted, all the voyage of their life
> Is bound in shallows and in miseries.
> On such a full sea are we now afloat,
> And we must take the current when it serves,
> Or lose our ventures.

While I don't think good timing can be taught, it can be learned. From the outside, and in retrospect, it always looks like good timing is little more than luck. In fact, it's a lot more than luck. It grows out of experience, doing your homework, and learning to trust your intuition.

● Problems are opportunities.

In fact, in China, the word *crisis* means "opportunity." It is only during the bad times that the true mettle of a man is tested. I learned nothing from my successes on Wall Street and everything from my failures. Likewise, it takes trouble to bring out the best—or worst—in our business partners. Until you've gone through crisis together, it's fair to say that you don't really know each other. Some, like Nick, pass that test brilliantly; others go to pieces and fail miserably.

● Don't sell yourself short.

Most of us assume that just because we don't have money in our pockets, we can't start a business. I didn't believe this when I started selling Christmas trees, Bernie didn't believe this when he got on the plane for Sweden, and Nick certainly didn't believe it when he developed his concept of Italian math. Don't you believe it either.

- ### Italian math.

One and one can equal much more than two. Just look at what happens when two lowly molecules of hydrogen meet one molecule of oxygen: water!

- ### Italian finance.

When you're starting out, never go to a bank to borrow money. It's trite, but true, that banks loan money only to those people who don't need it. Instead, go to people who know you and believe in you: your family, your suppliers, or your potential customers. If you do involve your customers, always offer them an ongoing discount to sweeten the deal.

- ### Italian profits.

Every business has a certain overhead, but once you break even, your percentage of profitability will increase disproportionately with every dollar of additional revenue. Put another way, recall that Nick made no profit when his sales were $175,000, and $400,000 profit when his sales were $800,000. In most businesses, margins increase dramatically after the overhead costs have been met.

- ### It's not so terrible not to be a winner in your twenties.

Remember, Nick was twenty-eight before he even got on the right boat to America, and Abe hadn't made his first million until he was forty. It took Vince Lombardi twenty-five years before he became head coach of a pro team.

Meatballs for Millions

Although there are certainly exceptions, I think that most people in their twenties are too immature and inexperienced to handle real financial success. Many athletes and most rock stars who hit it big early are broke by thirty or thirty-five. I think those years are better used preparing for *permanent* success.

- **Always do more than you're paid for, and soon you'll be paid for more than you do.**

Nick knew this intuitively, and today, it's even easier to do than it was in Nick's day because so many of us do less than we're paid for. To me, that sounds like an opportunity. If you do more, it's a pretty sure bet you'll be recognized almost immediately. If you are employed, and your boss just doesn't care, either go after his or her job or go looking for another company.

- **Pick your friends for their integrity, not for their money.**

Money is plentiful; good friends are rare.

Part Two

Applying the
Laws of
Success

Chapter 4

Getting Started

ONE OF THE difficulties in becoming an entrepreneur is that, until you've succeeded at least once, you really have to go about your work without the fueling effects of encouragement. Naysayers, doubters, and just plain negative thinkers are everywhere. Thousands of people told me why Visible Changes would never succeed. Hundreds of times I was advised to call it quits.

Being an entrepreneur is a particularly lonely pursuit because we have become what sociologist David Riesman calls an "outer-directed" society. That is to say that we get our sense of self-esteem and well-being from how loudly others applaud our actions. Almost no one applauds entrepreneurs until they succeed.

Therefore, the entrepreneur must look inward for support. The essential ingredients of entrepreneurship are a vision, a sense of mission, and a will to keep going forward when everyone else is telling you to go back.

In this chapter, I want to share with you some of my personal experiences in starting Visible Changes. It wasn't brains, brawn, or even our business plan that resulted in our ultimate success. It was persistence, pure and simple.

Author Tom Wolfe claims he can pick an FBI agent out of any crowd at a distance of a hundred feet. It's the squeaky black shoes, he says, that give them away.

Likewise, I can pick a banker out of any lineup: His shoes are wing tips, his shirt is usually white, and he still ties the old-fashioned Windsor knot, the fat one, in his tie. Of course, his suit is dark, pin-striped, and three-piece. If the banker is a woman, you can count on her wearing the floppy bow-tie that has been foisted upon her by the legion of "Dress for Success" authors.

The reason I'm an expert on the spotting, care, and feeding of bankers is that I had to deal with hundreds of them during my initial efforts to fund Visible Changes. For some reason, many businessmen in Texas, where we decided to start our company, are perfectly capable of riding the mechanical bull at a local saloon or staring down big game at close range, but quiver at the thought of having to deal with bankers. They even feel slightly uncomfortable around the panning surveillance cameras.

Getting over this fear, especially for fledgling entrepreneurs, is essential, since a good relationship with a banker is critical to most business start-ups.

For some reason I'll never understand, bankers love business plans with lots of numbers, five-year projections, analyses of the competition, anticipated marketing strategies, job descriptions, salaries, scenarios, and anything else you can cram in to make it appear as if you've done your homework. I've seen many business start-ups where the plan, in effect, becomes the product, and the entrepreneur encounters paralysis by analysis.

When we began Visible Changes, I was no exception to this rule. What began as a simple, comprehensive business plan became, over time, an elaborately detailed and lengthy study calculated to answer any question a banker or investor could possibly ask me. If you wanted to know what a water cooler would cost in our fifth year of operations, given certain inflation assumptions, I could go into my crammed briefcase and substantiate my answer.

In truth, while it is essential to think through the critical factors for the success or failure of any new business, most of this business plan stuff is pure bunk. The bankers want it to cover their own behinds, and most sophisticated investors don't even bother to read it. They'll look at a few key assumptions, consider the concept, examine the tax consequences, and make a determination as to whether the people involved can make it work. That's all.

But in 1976, when I hit the road trying to raise $500,000 to

Getting Started

get Visible Changes off the ground, I tried to impress people with the quantity of my research as well as its quality. My plan was to put in the $100,000 that Maryanne and I had managed to save from a beauty salon she had started in New York City, raise an additional $150,000 from private investors in exchange for 25 percent of the company, and fund the remaining $250,000 with a bank loan. The plan was to start two or three very fancy salons in the better shopping malls, build some cash flow, and expand from there.

The bankers, it turned out, loved my presentation, were intrigued with my diverse background, but hated the hairdressing industry. Several even offered to give me the quarter million if I'd go into an industry other than hairdressing. Why not a nice chain of Tex-Mex restaurants?, I was asked more than once.

What the bankers saw as limitations, I saw as possibilities. It was true that the hairdressing industry was one of the worst-managed mom-and-pop professions in the country. Nevertheless, even with those negative images, the numbers were encouraging. The industry, as a whole, was bringing in billions a year—everybody who had a head had to get a haircut—and this market wasn't going to go away. The very fact that the industry was so fractionated—no one chain did more than 1 percent of the business—looked to me like an opportunity. And the fact that there was virtually no enlightened management in the industry—no one was making use of advances in technology (especially the computer as a marketing tool)—led me to believe I was on the right track. Lastly, and not incidentally, Maryanne was a master haircutter herself who had run, hands-on, a very successful salon in New York City. It was that salon with its $80,000 in annual profits that became our main source of income during our early years.

And so, with my business plan in hand, I started knocking

on bankers' doors, usually dealing with the loan officers. The meetings lasted anywhere from thirty minutes to four hours, and they all had a common theme: The bankers liked me, they liked my plan, but they thought hairdressers were flaky, unstable, or worse. They all said no. On some days I'd make as many as three or four presentations, literally getting dizzy and forgetting what I had already told to whom. It was a marathon.

Bankers are, by their nature, conservative bean-counters, and entrepreneurs are, by definition, risk-taking bean-planters. I'll make my point simply: can you point out a banker or a bookkeeper who has ever started anything on his or her own—other than trouble?

The lending institutions in this country are bureaucratically stacked against the entrepreneur or the original thinker, and our country's economy is paying dearly for it. Bankers love to write checks to companies with track records, because they don't have to do any work to do it, but as we can well document here in Texas—the bank-failure capital of the country—many of those "safe loans" made in the last decade have been nothing short of foolhardy. To this day, I worry more about my bank going broke than I do about myself going broke.

After the 265th bank had turned me down, I called Maryanne in New York and told her I was quitting. I couldn't do it, I was giving up. We'd try something else. The Tex-Mex restaurants were sounding better and better.

Maryanne, who is wise in all things—but especially wise to my antics—said something like, "Yes, I understand, dear. Two hundred sixty-five banks. You must feel terrible, and I know you're exhausted. If you want to quit, you know I'll stand by you. Of course, you know, dear, Walt and Mickey didn't quit and didn't succeed until the three hundred and third bank."

It was true. Walt Disney was one of my heroes, and Mickey,

Getting Started

of course, was his yet-to-be born mouse. Disney had been turned down by three hundred two banks before he found a banker who believed in him and his idea enough to help him get started.

I went back on the road and received a message that a banker in Dallas could meet me at 2:30 P.M. the following day. I was in Houston, and I was wary, because the only seat I could get was first-class on an American Airlines flight, and my cash supply had dwindled to almost nothing. The first-class airfare was $125. It was, at the time, a major decision. I decided to go for it.

Don Weckwerth, chairman of a small bank in Fort Worth, met me at Dallas/Fort Worth Airport, and we did our business over a table in a cafeteria. About thirty minutes into my presentation, Weckwerth said he'd never seen more garbage in his life: numbers, charts, projections, assumptions, the whole nine yards. "How much do you need?" he asked. I told him $250,000, explaining that I had $100,000 of my own money and intended to raise $150,000 from investors in exchange for 25 percent of the company.

Weckwerth didn't like that at all. "Get rid of the investors," he said, "keep 100 percent of the business for yourself, and I'll get you $250,000 for the first two salons." If they were successful, we could use those two as collateral for the next ones. I told him I liked the idea.

"Who's your lawyer?" he asked.

I told him I didn't have one, but I'd be happy to use his. That would be unethical, he said. "Recommend two," I said. "I want you to be totally comfortable with me." Weckwerth said he'd be totally comfortable after I signed on the dotted line, because I was going to guarantee the loan personally with every asset I had.

I had no problem with that, but I wanted him to know up front that I didn't have much. I was, however, 100 percent committed. In this high-wire act, there were to be no nets. I'm always skeptical—and so are investors—of businesspeople who hedge their bets or plan to live high on the hog. They want their payoff on the front end—exactly the opposite approach I had learned from Abe and Bernie and Nick.

My first call, from the airport, of course, went to Maryanne: "I can't believe it. We got it!" She couldn't believe it either, but we were in business.

Well, not quite. Nothing in real life, especially in finance, ever goes smoothly, and our deal was no exception. First, our loan was to be a Small Business Administration loan, and that meant loads of paperwork had to be completed and submitted by a certain deadline. This was especially important, because the deadline— noon on a Friday—was the end of one fiscal quarter and the start of another. If we were even five minutes late, we'd have to redo all of our projections and paperwork.

For two days and two nights, my accountant David Stovall (another person I met through Weckwerth) and I holed up in a Dallas hotel room, filling out the required reports and forms. We bribed a temporary secretary to keep up with us on the typing, and I literally ran into the post office to get our envelope postmarked. It was five minutes before noon. To this day, although I've had many opportunities to switch to a Big Eight accounting firm, I still do, and always will do, business with David Stovall. He was there with me in the beginning when I most needed his help.

Several years later, in recognition of Don Weckwerth, the only banker who would take a chance on Visible Changes, we honored him as Banker of the Year at Houston's huge Summit Auditorium. It was Visible Changes night at a Houston Rockets game, and I had bought seats for our company behind one of the baskets. I invited Weckwerth to come to the game, but he had no idea he was the honoree.

We picked him up at the airport in a limousine and ushered

Getting Started

him into the Summit where I told him it was his duty to give a little talk at halftime and present Rockets center Moses Malone with an award. Weckwerth said fine, and when he got to midcourt with Malone and the microphone, banners fell from the rafters honoring him as "Banker of the Year." Weckwerth almost fell over with surprise. We gave him a plaque and a gold Rolex watch, which I had inscribed, "For seeing the reality, when it was only a dream!"

That reality began in Houston when we started construction for the first Visible Changes at the popular Greenspoint Mall, in Houston. Although we were located at the dead end of a corridor, I wanted to build a showplace. Ordinarily, salons were built like prisons with little cells out of sight of everyone, as if something secretive or suspect were going on in the back room.

At our salon, we took the opposite approach: We wanted our haircutters to think of themselves as artists, and we wanted to give them a platform on which to perform. We began with a fifty-foot picture window facing the mall, theatrical track lighting, and a raised stage where our haircutters performed. Our color scheme, on the advice of a team of psychologists, was high-tech black and white, softened only by judiciously placed green earth-tones. Everything in our salon, from our stereo system to our furnishings, was to be first-class.

Most of the "chains" that had attempted to do business in Houston offered cheap surroundings, poorly trained haircutters, and shabby service. It makes mathematical sense: If you're charging only six dollars for a haircut, there is no way you can pay a decent wage to decent haircutters, and eventually they'll quit and move on. I believed then, and I believe more than ever now, that haircutters are indeed professionals who probably have more to do with how you look than your tailor, and they need to be well trained—and well paid.

Applying the Laws of Success

I was putting into practice what I had learned from Nick, my caterer friend: people will gladly pay higher prices for higher quality, better service, and a pleasant experience in pleasant surroundings.

We built our first and second salon ourselves, and practically simultaneously. Greenspoint opened on October 6, 1977, and the Sharpstown Mall location on the day after Thanksgiving. Maryanne and I put up the wallpaper ourselves on Thanksgiving Day, because no one else would help us on a holiday. Two of our employees brought us a smoked turkey, and we cut it with our only utensil, a wallpaper penknife.

At that point, Maryanne asked, "Are we crazy?" I said I didn't know, but I did know that we couldn't open without wallpaper, and we worked all night to finish the job. The next day, the busiest day in the mall the entire year, we held our grand opening. We did a total of three haircuts.

Although to this day I remind Maryanne that I never promised her a rose garden, what she did in those early years was superhuman. We had decided not to take any salary out of Visible Changes for at least two years, pouring our profits, if any, into paying off our debt and opening more salons. Therefore, our only income was coming from her New York salon, which she continued to operate.

Typically, she'd close her New York salon at seven o'clock on Saturday night, and quickly do payroll and inventory so they could order supplies the following Tuesday (the salon was closed Sunday and Monday). She'd then race out to LaGuardia Airport in a cab to catch a 9 P.M. flight to Houston, where she'd arrive at 11:30 P.M. We'd then go to the only restaurant open near Greenspoint, a Denny's, and talk until about three-thirty in the morning about what was happening here and there. Then we'd go home for a couple hours' sleep, and at 9 A.M. on Sunday,

Getting Started

Maryanne would arrive at the salon and teach class to new hair-cutters at the salon until 6 P.M., while I worked mainly on construction. She taught Sunday, Monday, Tuesday, and most of the day Wednesday before catching a 9 P.M. flight back to New York, which would arrive at 3:15 in the morning. By 7 A.M., she'd be at her New York salon and work until 7 P.M. She put in similar twelve-hour days on Friday and Saturday, and then repeat the cycle. She did this for nine months.

Three weeks after we opened Greenspoint, disaster struck. A water heater in a closet had overheated, and when Maryanne opened the closet door, flames exploded out into the salon. A fireman who happened to be getting his hair cut dashed into the mall and returned with a hand-held fire extinguisher. He sprayed the place down with a white, powdery substance, but the damage was already done.

When I arrived around 8 P.M., unaware of any problem, the mall manager was waiting for me. He thought I had purposely torched my own place, since the business was obviously such a loser. At best, he said, if I wanted to rebuild, I'd be out of business for a month.

"Not a chance," I said. "I'll be open for business as usual at 10 A.M. tomorrow. You might want to stop by for a haircut." I had a lot more fire in my belly than I had had in my salon.

I immediately called my brother-in-law, who was working at Sharpstown, and told him of the emergency. "Grab everybody you can from Sharpstown. Call plumbers, painters, electricians, carpenters, and get them over here tonight. Tell them I'll bonus each of them two hundred dollars, but they've got to work all night."

About thirty workers showed up, and they really got into the spirit of the thing. They ripped out the charred Sheetrock, repaired the wiring and the plumbing, replastered, repainted, and completely cleaned that white-powder mess from every inch of the salon. By daybreak, they were exhausted, but ebullient. I've never seen a prouder bunch of workers in my life!

At 10 A.M., sure enough, the mall manager was there to see us open our doors, and I'd pay ten thousand dollars today if I could have captured the look on his face in a photograph.

"You've accomplished a miracle," he allowed, and in a way, I guess we had, but he added, "I still don't think you've got a chance in hell of making this place work."

Now I've already indicated to you that I learned some pretty impressive lessons in persistence from Bernie (remember the Sweden story) and Nick (the toothbrush-in-the-bathroom story), but nothing in my past prepared me for dealing with a woman I'll call Ann, once portrayed in *Texas Monthly* magazine as the piranha of real estate mavens.

I can't overemphasize the importance of high-traffic mall locations to the success of Visible Changes. Our initial problem wasn't just that these locations were in many cases prohibitively expensive, but that the mall managers didn't want hair salons in the first place. Unless I could break that barrier, Visible Changes, as I envisaged it, didn't stand a chance.

Ann, I soon learned, was the key person. She represented many of the top malls in Texas, and she had one, in particular, we wanted to be in: Valley View Mall in Dallas.

I walked into Ann's office unannounced, and her secretary asked if I had an appointment. No, I said, but I'd wait. I sat down and started reading magazines. Two hours later, the secretary said Ann would see me at two o'clock the following day. I continued to sit. Finally, the piranha herself came out and asked what I was doing there. Finishing up an article, I replied. Two o'clock tomorrow, she said curtly, and disappeared.

The next day, at 1 P.M., I was back at her office. At two on the button, Ann appeared and was most gracious, but to the point:

Getting Started

"What can I do for you, Mr. McCormack? You have five minutes. I'm very busy."

I explained quickly my concept for Visible Changes and she said, "That's very nice, but I have no interest. Good day, Mr. McCormack."

The next morning, a Wednesday, at 9 A.M., I was back. The secretary asked what I wanted. I told her I had gotten only five minutes the day before, but that I had an hour-long story. I wanted her to put me down for five minutes a day until the end of the month.

Again, Ann appeared in the waiting room. She told me she totally understood my deal and that she had absolutely no interest in beauty salons in her malls. I protested that I really hadn't had the time to inform her fully of my plans, and, finally, she relented. She said, "I'll make you a deal, Mr. McCormack. . . ."

"Call me John."

"Mr. McCormack, I'll see you for fifteen minutes on Friday if you don't come back here on Thursday." We shook on it.

On Friday I gave her a longer presentation, and she gave me a shorter answer: No way.

Monday morning, of course, I was back in the waiting room, and I overheard her secretary tell Ann, "He's back."

"What now?" the piranha asked.

"I need an hour," I told her. "I'm obviously not explaining my concept well enough, so I need more time." I thought she was beginning to like me.

The following Friday I spent an hour with Ann. I explained to her why Visible Changes was exactly what she needed in her malls to increase pedestrian traffic and to add a little bit of pizzazz and glamour. I didn't see how she could resist.

I was wrong. She almost had me believing that she really meant it when she said no, but I wasn't quite ready to give up.

I called Maryanne and asked her to get on a plane on Sunday and come on down. At eight o'clock Monday morning, Maryanne and I were in Ann's waiting room. The secretary, at this point, had gotten into the game, and started laughing hysterically. Fifteen minutes later, Ann walked in and turned beet red. She started, "Mr. McCormack, I've told you. . . ."

That was about as far as she got before I said, "I want you to meet my wife, Maryanne. I asked Maryanne to fly in from New York so she could critique what I'm doing wrong with my presentation. If you could just see us both together for ten minutes anytime within the next three days—when she has to be back at work—we'd be forever grateful." Ann laughed and invited us in for fifteen minutes.

So again, I made my pitch in front of Maryanne, and Ann said directly to Maryanne that I had made a great presentation, there was absolutely nothing wrong with it, she understood the concept, but she also had no interest in any haircutting operations in any of her malls. It was a friendly conversation, and I'm sure Ann thought it was our final conversation.

Now, it so happened that there was an upcoming convention of mall managers in Las Vegas, and that you had to call the managers in advance to make appointments. I called Ann and got her secretary. She started laughing. "We don't think you're dangerous," she said, "but we do think you're crazy. What do you want?"

"An appointment with Ann in Las Vegas."

"Forget it," she said. "You're history. I'd lose my job. You're out."

I let a little time pass and called back. I'm not bad at disguising my voice, and I began: "This is Mr. McDougal, John McDougal, from California. I have a new line of women's wear, and I need about fifteen hundred square feet in a prime mall location. I do

Getting Started

about a half-million per store. I'd like to visit with Ann while I'm at the mall convention in Las Vegas."

Fine, said the secretary, and she set up the appointment.

A few days later, Maryanne and I flew to Las Vegas and went straight to the hospitality suite that Ann's company had rented in one of the major hotels. A number of people were milling around in the anteroom, and I tried to look inconspicuous.

Ann's secretary spotted me immediately. She told me I'd better get out of there because if Ann saw me, there was going to be trouble. She might even call security. In fact, said the secretary, Ann specifically went over her list of appointments to be sure I wasn't on it. And, said the secretary as the clincher, Ann is booked solid with appointments. There were no openings.

Just at that moment, Ann herself walked into the room, and spotted me at the bar. She came at me like a barracuda, a slight upgrade from the piranha image she had cultivated, and said, "Mr. McCormack . . ." And I said, "Ann, I can't believe you picked me out of all these people in this room. This is unbelievable . . .," and she cut me off.

"Mr. McCormack, enough with the flowers. It's very nice to see you here, have a drink, but I have no time to see you because I'm fully booked."

I said, "Yes, I know."

"How do you know that?" she asked.

I replied that I had tried to make an appointment, but her efficient secretary had told me she was booked. However, I went on, I had a friend, John McDougal, who was downstairs and needed to cancel his appointment. "He'll call you in a few days, but in the meantime, he said I could take his time."

Ann, of course, knew this was baloney. "You wait right here," she said.

She returned in a few minutes with a whole group of VIPs,

pointed at me, and said, "He's the guy I've been telling you about."

"You mean, I'm famous before my time?" I said. "I can't believe it. And I haven't even opened my store in Ann's mall yet." They got into the spirit of the thing, asked me about my idea, and then told Ann, "Gee, it sounds pretty good. Why don't you give him a chance." I then said, "C'mon Ann, what difference does it make if I do $300,000 in dresses or $300,000 in hair?"

She didn't melt, but she did relent. "Okay," she said, "I can't put you in Dallas, but I can put you in Houston. We're opening a center down there called Baybrook in nine months. This is where I'll put you," and she pointed on a diagram to a terrible location near a remote, low-traffic entrance. I thanked her profusely and walked out with Maryanne, who was skeptical.

"John," she said, "we might as well be at the dead end of some hallway. It will never work."

"Maryanne," I said, "I spent a month listening to noes. At least let's celebrate this yes, and then we'll figure out how to upgrade our location later."

That upgrade, in fact, didn't prove too difficult. After we opened our first salon at Greenspoint, I invited Ann down for a look, and she was awed. She immediately gave me a better location at Baybrook, which continues to be one of our better stores. To this day, I continue to do a lot of business with Ann.

Several years after our first encounters, she came back to me and asked why I had been so much of a pest in the beginning. "Ann," I told her, "what was being a pest to you was a matter of survival—almost life or death—to me. It was my business, my only shot. I tried to add some humor to what I was doing, but it was very serious business for me."

The key, of course, is self-confidence. You've got to believe in yourself and what you're doing, and then, simply and completely,

Getting Started

go for it. Regardless of what the piranhas of this world will tell you, they appreciate persistence, and persistence works.

Action Plan

- **Look inward, not outward, for support and encouragement.**

It's been estimated that by the time we reach the age of five, we've been programmed with more than twenty-five thousand hours of "tapes," most of them negative ("Not in this house you don't." "Wipe that smile off your face." "You've had enough fun for now." "Where did you ever get such a crazy idea?", etc.). These messages continually replay in our minds and are reinforced by our well-meaning friends, who have been similarly programmed. The entrepreneur must identify with his vision so strongly and completely that these negative tapes are subsumed by the pure force of belief in an idea. I've found that in the incubation stage of a venture, it's usually better to keep my dreams to myself and to keep my own counsel until my idea becomes strong enough to withstand the inevitable criticism from outside forces.

- **Hold on to your vision.**

Nearly everyone with whom you share your dream will attempt to alter it, if only slightly, with his or her own input. This is especially true of investors or bankers who feel they have a proprietary right to influence their investment. My best advice is to resist compromising your vision, even if it does mean looking elsewhere for funding. Mickey Mouse could very easily have turned into a lap poodle if Walt Disney had listened to his investors (just as Visible Changes could have turned into a chain of Tex-Mex restaurants).

- **Practice "goal-oriented thinking."**

Before entering into a transaction or even making a telephone call, be clear in your own mind what you're trying to accomplish. Entrepreneurs are prone to misinterpret "good conversation" or "good feeling" for real progress toward an identifiable goal.

- **Use your personality as a business tool.**

If people like you, they'll help you. Humor will help you through difficult situations. Ann would never have put up with my antics if she hadn't been getting a bit of a kick out of my behavior. I was so persistent, and so outrageous, that she couldn't help herself from helping me.

- **Be willing to sign on the line for personal liability.**

The first time out of the box, bet everything. After all, it's your venture so why shouldn't it be your risk? (Besides, you don't have that much to lose.) After you have achieved your first success, however, take yourself off the line and protect yourself by letting your lenders take the risk. You've already done your part by proving yourself, thereby reducing their risk.

- **Do not take no for an answer.**

Having children under age five, I constantly see how often they will ask for the same thing over and over again, regardless of how many times I tell them no. And yet, as we grow older, we learn to accept the very first no. Always try to avoid a direct confrontation, because as long as you're getting noes, you'll still be in the game. The idea is to turn noes into maybes and maybes into yesses.

- **If you can avoid it, don't take in partners, and never take in a partner for his or her money, only for his or her intelligence or expertise.**

When I first met my banker, Don Weckwerth, I was planning to raise money by selling 5 percent shares in Visible Changes for

Getting Started

$20,000 each. He convinced me that this might prove to be a very costly plan, and he was right. Today those shares would have been worth millions. If your idea is going to work, do not sell ownership in it cheap at the outset—even if it looks like easy money.

- **Reward your staff with profits, not stock.**

Once you bring in shareholders, the government can come in, take a look at everything you're doing, and start telling you how to run your business. And, I can guarantee you, the government knows nothing about running a business.

- **The cheapest is not always the best, and people do look for quality.**

There is so much junk out there in the marketplace that quality and service stand out today more than ever. The American consumer is tired of junk and shoddy workmanship and is willing to pay a premium for better goods and services. Mark my words: the movement in the nineties will be back toward excellence.

Chapter 5

Conation

SEVERAL YEARS AGO at the Harvard Business School, the students gathered together to collectively "let their hair down." For weeks the students had been interviewing with the scions of Fortune 500 companies who make their annual spring pilgrimage to the Cambridge campus on the banks of the Charles River to entice the best and brightest budding capitalists into their executive training programs.

While the process conjures up images of power brokers doing power lunches at fashionable restaurants and watering holes, the reality is that long before a recruit gets to this stage, he or she must first get past the initial rite that takes place in a prisonlike little cell of an office. It is the introductory interview. On average, each candidate has only thirty minutes to sell him- or herself to the recruiter, who, again on average, will visit with eight to ten students in a day.

Likewise, during recruiting season, the students, too, will visit with a half-dozen or so different companies and, by day's end, neither the recruiters nor the recruits remember exactly what they have said to whom. It's a dizzying process, made all the more dizzying because nearly all of the Harvard Business School résumés read remarkably alike.

All of the students were graduated at the top of their high school class, many were valedictorians, most had 4.0 averages in college, and all had excelled in business before deciding to go on to take their MBA degree. For hobbies, they enjoy backgammon and skiing, and, of course, all have traveled extensively throughout Europe.

The irony of this homogeneity of excellence, it seems, is not lost on the students themselves, and therefore, the more creative among them each year put together an evening of student skits to let off some of the pressure and, well, just cut up. On the particular year in question, the students had composed a little musical number entitled, "Am I My Résumé?"

The question is a provocative one: Do all of the degrees, grades, prizes, experiences, honors, and awards form a mosaic that adds up to an accurate portrait of a person, and, even more important to a potential employer, do they predict with any accuracy how well an individual will perform once he or she gets the keys to the executive washroom?

A substantial body of evidence is being compiled that suggests they do not. In fact, employers have been jamming so many round pegs into so many square holes for so long in corporate America that we now have a work force in place that, for the most part, hates its job and demonstrates that dislike with the lowest productivity rate in the industrialized world, coupled with the highest rate of worker transience. Company loyalty, for the most part, is nonexistent.

Why are we so inept at producing employee satisfaction and predicting employee success? I believe it's because we're asking the wrong questions and looking at the wrong indicators. Yes, past success, test scores, personality profiles, and other personnel-screening techniques may offer some clues, but they don't measure what I believe is the most important innate indicator of success, and that is *conation*.

Simply put, conation is the will to succeed, the quest for success, the attitude that "to stop me you'll have to kill me," that elusive "fire in the belly" that manifests itself in drive, enthusiasm, excitement, and single-mindedness in pursuit of a goal—any goal. All consistently successful people have it. Many well-educated, intelligent, endearing, and presentable people don't have it.

Since I was familiar with this concept for some time and had

Conation

read somewhere that *conation* was one of the more obscure words in the English language (as well as one of the most important), I was delighted to learn that an author, Kathy Kolbe, had just written an entire book on the subject, entitled *The Conative Connection*, published by Addison-Wesley. I'd like to share a more complete definition of conation from Kolbe's book, which she cites from *The 1,000 Most Obscure Words in the English Language*.

> **Conation** (koh NAY shun) n. Conation is the area of one's active mentality that has to do with desire, volition, and striving. The related **conatus** (koh NAY tus) is the resulting effort or striving itself, or the natural tendency or force in one's mental makeup that produces an effort. **Conative** (KOHN uh tiv) is the term in psychology that describes anything relating to conation. All these words come from the Latin conatus, past participle of the verb conari (to try). . . . Conation differs from velleity (the wish without the effort).

I'm not sure that any of us yet knows how to measure accurately the amount of will or drive or need-to-succeed of any individual, but I know some people just can't be stopped, regardless of the odds or the obstacles, and these are the people one should never bet against.

Social or economic background seems to have little to do with conation. Robert Kennedy and Martin Luther King, Jr., had it, as does Lee Iacocca, Donald Trump, or anyone who keeps coming back, fighting back, getting off the canvas, and getting on with his or her mission.

To illustrate the concept of conation in real-life terms, I'd like to share with you three short stories of three very different people in my life, each of whom had seemingly insurmountable problems. They also had conation.

Applying the Laws of Success

The first is Le Van Vu, a Vietnamese immigrant who has gone on to make millions in this country; the second is Tony Hatty, a tough kid out of Detroit who had given up on the hairdressing industry forever—until he joined Visible Changes and became the top haircutter in America; and the third is Steven Waldon, a black haircutter for us who was headed for real trouble until he took stock in himself, realized he had something to offer the world, and went on to make something of himself.

When Maryanne and I were building our Greenspoint Mall salon thirteen years ago, a Vietnamese fellow would stop by each day to sell us doughnuts. He spoke hardly any English, but he was always friendly, and, through smiles and sign language, we got to know each other. His name was Le Van Vu.

During the day, Le worked in a bakery, and at night he and his wife listened to audiotapes to learn English. I later learned that they slept on sacks full of sawdust on the floor of the back room of the bakery.

In Vietnam, the Van Vu family was one of the wealthiest in Southeast Asia. They owned almost one-third of North Vietnam, including huge holdings in industry and in real estate. However, after his father was brutally murdered, Le moved to South Vietnam with his mother, where he went to school and eventually became a lawyer.

Like his father before him, Le prospered. He saw an opportunity to construct buildings to accommodate the ever-expanding American presence in South Vietnam and soon became one of the most successful builders in the country.

On a trip to the North, however, Le was captured by the North Vietnamese and thrown into prison for three years. He escaped by killing five soldiers and made his way back to South Vietnam

Conation

where again he was arrested. The South Vietnamese government had assumed he was a "plant" from the North.

After serving time in prison, Le got out and started a fishing company, eventually becoming the largest canner in South Vietnam.

However, when Le learned that the U.S. troops and embassy personnel were about to pull out of his country, he made a life-changing decision.

He took all of the gold he had hoarded, loaded it aboard one of his fishing vessels, and sailed with his wife out to the American ships in the harbor. He then exchanged all his riches for safe passage out of Vietnam to the Philippines, where he and his wife were taken into a refugee camp. After gaining access to the president of the Philippines, Le convinced him to make one of his boats available for fishing and, again, Le was back in business. Before he left the Philippines two years later en route for America (his ultimate dream), Le had successfully developed the entire fishing industry in the Philippines.

Nevertheless, en route to America, Le became distraught and depressed about having to start over once again with nothing. His wife tells of how she found him near the railing of the ship, about to jump overboard. "Le," she told him, "if you do jump, what ever will become of me? We've been together for so long and through so much. We can do this together."

It was all the encouragement that Le Van Vu needed. Like Abe and Nick and Bernie before him, Le, too, decided to fight one more time.

When he and his wife arrived in Houston in 1972, they were flat broke and spoke no English. In Vietnam, however, family takes care of family, and Le and his wife found themselves ensconced in the back room of his cousin's bakery in the Greenspoint Mall. We were building our salon just a couple hundred feet away.

Now, as they say, here comes the "message" part of this story:

Le's cousin offered both Le and his wife jobs in the bakery. After taxes, Le would take home $175 per week, his wife $125. Their total annual income, in other words, was $15,600. Further, his cousin offered to sell them the bakery whenever they could come up with a $30,000 down payment. The cousin would finance the remainder with a note for $90,000.

Here's what Le and his wife did:

Even with a weekly income of $300, they decided to continue to live in the back room. They kept clean by taking sponge baths for two years in the mall's restrooms. For two years their diet consisted almost entirely of bakery goods. Each year, for two years, they lived on a total, that's right, a *total* of $600, saving $30,000 for the down payment.

Le later explained to me his reasoning: "If we got ourselves an apartment, which we could afford on $300 per week, we'd have to pay the rent. Then, of course, we'd have to buy furniture. Then we'd have to have transportation to and from work, so that meant we'd have to buy a car. Then we'd have to buy gasoline for the car as well as insurance. Then we'd probably want to go places in the car, so that meant we'd need to buy clothes and toiletries. So I knew that if we got that apartment, we'd never get our $30,000 together."

Now, if you think you've heard everything about Le, let me tell you, there's more: After he and his wife had saved the $30,000 and bought the bakery, Le once again sat down with his wife for a serious chat. They still owed $90,000 to his cousin, he said, and as difficult as the past two years had been, they had to remain living in that back room for one more year.

I'm proud to tell you that in one year, my friend and mentor Le Van Vu and his wife, saving virtually every nickel of profit from the business, paid off the $90,000 note, and in just three years, owned an extremely profitable business free and clear.

Conation

Then, and only then, the Van Vu's went out and got their first apartment. To this day, they continue to save on a regular basis, live on an extremely small percentage of their income, and, of course, always pays cash for any of their purchases.

Do you think that Le Van Vu is a millionaire today? I am happy to tell you, many times over.

As I write these words, Le is in the process of starting or acquiring six substantial companies. Newspapers and magazines have written articles on the "miracle" of Le Van Vu. Recently he met with the deans of several major business schools at my house, and they were in awe of what Le has been able to accomplish with his life—again and again. The key is conation.

As I travel from university to university, spreading my message of self-sacrifice, saving, discipline, and hard work, I sometimes ask Le Van Vu to accompany me as a living example of what sacrifice really means. His English is not perfect, and he always apologizes to his audiences for that, but by the end of his talk, the students are mesmerized. They've never even met anyone with Le Van Vu's will to succeed—and his willingness to save and sacrifice, a willingness that assures success.

I think role models like Le ought to be teaching in every school in America. The bad news is that now that America is truly part of a global economy, the Le Van Vu's of this world are now the competition. How would you like to put a pampered graduate of an elite business school up against Le in a do-or-die business deal? I'll tell you where I'd put my money.

Now let me tell you about Tony Hatty, the top hairdresser in the United States in 1988 according to *American Salon* magazine.

When Tony first came to Texas in 1981 from Detroit, Michigan (so many people were leaving Detroit for Houston, there were bumper stickers on cars saying, WILL THE LAST PERSON WHO LEAVES

MICHIGAN PLEASE TURN OUT THE LIGHTS), he was desperate. Nothing was working for Tony Hatty in life.

Born into an ethnic family in Detroit—a hardworking Lebanese father and a Polish mother who ran a neighborhood grocery store until somebody burned it down in 1971—Tony found his popularity in life and in school by being the goof-off, the screwup, the class clown. He hated school, his grades reflected it, and he was on a first-name basis with the principal for all the wrong reasons.

As he got older, his hair got longer and his behavior got worse: he took uppers, downers, some marijuana. During high school, he job-hopped and had probably the longest résumé for a teenager in the Motor City: thirty to forty jobs, including stints at a pizza joint, a burger joint, a clothing store, and even the Ford Motor Company.

When his girlfriend suggested beauty school, he decided to try it ("Why not? I'll try anything three times!"), and he surprised himself by liking it and actually being pretty good at it. He looked at his diploma as a passport, and it was—to frustration. In a short period, he had added twelve more entries—all salons—to his résumé. He had never worked harder in his life, and he had never been more broke. Tony concluded, "There's no money in hair, and there's no future for me in Detroit." He was right on both counts. The city had a 28 percent unemployment rate, his W-2 form for the previous year showed $4,500 in income, and he was collecting food stamps to stay alive.

Then Tony found a copy of *The Houston Post*, thick as a phone book and swollen with help-wanted ads, in a Detroit bookstore. "What am I doing here?" Tony asked himself. Even more so, "What am I doing with my life? I'm not going to settle for this. I'm going to Houston!"

Thus began the Tony Hatty odyssey, not unreminiscent of my

Conation

immigrant friends who had to leave their homelands for opportunities elsewhere.

Tony sold his most prized possessions to finance the trip: his stereo, his Beatles albums, and most of his personal belongings. He piled what he couldn't sell into the back of his broken-down Volkswagen and, at 2:30 A.M. on a snowy Detroit morning, kissed and hugged his mother and father good-bye on the front porch of their home. Everyone was crying.

Three days later, Tony arrived in Houston and recalls seeing a sign on the freeway. It had about fourteen arrows going every which way. Thought Tony, "It's like my life!"

Like Le Van Vu, Tony at first couldn't afford an apartment—Houston was booming at the time and the entry fee was a two-month security deposit—so he slept in his Volkswagen, washed up at gas station restrooms, and rationed his food money by eating fast food.

Now don't misunderstand me. Tony Hatty is a charmer—some might even say a hustler—and that's probably how he had gotten away with all the nonsense he had been involved with most of his life. So it is no surprise that he put those skills to good use and finally convinced an apartment manager to let him move into a little efficiency apartment and pay the bills as soon as he found meaningful work. His conation was beginning to show.

He had promised himself that he'd never do hair again, but he needed a haircut himself to go job hunting (some haircutters actually can cut their own hair, but Tony wasn't one of them), so he found his way to our Visible Changes in the Sharpstown Mall. The only problem was he didn't have the money for a haircut, but Tony was flabbergasted at what he saw: thirty people in line waiting for haircuts.

To Tony, it looked like a gold mine, a circus, Hollywood, but even more important, an opportunity. He spent the entire day on a bench outside our store and counted more than three hundred customers filing through. This definitely was not Detroit. He came back the following Monday, dressed in his best (and only) suit, and asked the manager what it took to get a job. A license and experience, she told him. He told her he had both, and she hired him on the spot.

Like everyone else in our company, Tony began as a trainee in the back room, shampooing hair, sweeping floors, and selling retail products. He was making $125 a week plus commission on his retail sales. Tony did the math quickly and decided that the secret to making money at Visible Changes was selling retail.

Says Tony: "There were seven of us training in the back room. I watched everybody trying to sell retail. They all did it the same way: they'd ask the customers if they needed any products, or if they wanted a conditioner on their hair. The customers would all say no.

"I said to myself, 'The thing they are all doing wrong is that they're asking the customer a yes-or-no question.

"Then I came up with a foolproof plan to sell retail. I didn't want the other trainees to hear me, so I turned on the water to muffle my voice. Then I would get down into the customer's ear and tell them, 'Welcome to my office. I am going to give you a great shampoo today,' and I'd get them all pumped up. Everybody in Houston had dry hair from the humidity, the chlorine, the sun, etc. I would tell them that I noticed that their hair was kind of dry, ask them if they swam a lot, and told them I could take care of that with any one of several conditioners.

"There was a hot towel treatment for $3 or another treatment for $5. 'Which one would you like?' I asked them.

"It worked! I'll never forget it. My first check in the back room (for two weeks' work) was about $400. My next one was $500. So, all of a sudden, I was making $250 a week, which was more than some of the new cutters. I was thinking that once I had

Conation

graduated to cutting and selling at the same time, I was going to be rich."

I first met Tony Hatty personally on a Saturday during my rounds to salons. He stepped right up to me, looked me in the eye, introduced himself, and told me how proud he was to be working at Visible Changes. He said he couldn't believe that some haircutters were complaining because they had too much work and told me about his days in Detroit when he considered himself lucky to do thirty haircuts in a week.

I knew what he was talking about. Desperation has a way of changing one's perspective.

From that point on, I began to hear stories of Tony Hatty that now have become lore and legend at Visible Changes. His manager told me he "loved to sweep the floors" and would always whistle or sing while he did it. People thought he was weird or wired or both, but, in fact, he was neither. He was on a roll—and still is.

In 1988, Tony was named "Hairstylist of the Year" by *American Salon* magazine, and for three consecutive years was our top producer in retail sales, our top hairstylist in terms of overall sales, and the recipient of just about every award, reward, cash bonus, company trip, and prize we can give out. He currently divides his time between his haircutting duties and traveling around the country giving motivational talks and sales seminars to large audiences.

He makes about a hundred grand a year, is in the process of putting in a pool at his new home, and, yes, can still be found most of the time cutting hair, sweeping, and whistling and singing at his station at our salon at the West Oaks Mall.

If you think Tony Hatty had a shaky beginning, let me introduce you to Steven Waldon, another one of our stars, born black and brought up in Houston, where racial prejudice was a fact of his

Applying the Laws of Success

daily life. Steven was headed for real trouble before he took responsibility for his own life.

I'll be frank with you. I had my doubts about Steven at first, and he had doubts about me. He thought that Visible Changes had a racial problem, and I thought he had an attitude problem. Maybe we both were right.

Steven was born into a large, close family, headed up by a no-nonsense father who wanted better things for his children than he had for himself, and a nurturing mother who was always there for him. The currency in the household to receive recognition, privileges, and pats on the back was good grades in school and good performance in sports, and Steven excelled in both areas. He ran track, played tennis, and participated in ROTC.

His father was a strict disciplinarian who was tough on himself and tough on his children, and even though Steven was surrounded by temptations, he usually resisted them simply because he was afraid of what his father would do if he found out.

Nevertheless, it was during high school that things began to go wrong for Steven Waldon, and even to this day he doesn't know why. He just began to lose interest in the things he used to be good at and enjoy—sports, studies, even his longtime friends. Life seemed to be losing its meaning—and its joy. He started doing just enough to get by, and, probably because of his upbringing, he felt guilty about it and terrible about himself. Always a winner, he was becoming in his own mind a loser.

Then, as people will do, he began to act more and more like the loser he felt he was until he eventually found himself face to face with a very serious, even deadly, situation. A new family had moved into his neighborhood, and the local bully started picking on Steven's new friend. Steven told his pal not to worry, that he would handle the situation, and he recalled some advice his father had once given him: "If you get into trouble with a really bad guy, you might as well kill him." And Steven decided to do just that.

Conation

He went home, got his sister's gun, loaded it, and went out in search of the bully. Steven Waldon was about to commit murder.

Call it divine intervention or whatever, but God was good to Steven that day—and good to the bully, who was nowhere to be found. Once Steven had calmed down, he began to ask himself the same questions that Tony Hatty did in Detroit: What am I doing with my life? What am I becoming? Don't I have more to offer the world than this?

In Steven's case, he surveyed his circle of friends and admitted that they all looked like and, in many cases, acted like, thugs. He decided he was worth more and enrolled in Lamar University.

I'd like to tell you that things went smoothly for Steven after that, but this is not a fairy tale. He stayed and studied (only halfheartedly) for three years before his father got fed up with him and told him if he wasn't going to apply himself, he might was well come home to work with him on the truck rig. The family needed the money, since his sister had come down with a paralysis-causing disease, and Steven's mother had to quit her job to care for her.

For a while, he worked in a pipe yard but got fired for sleeping on the job. He then became a security guard at a luxury high-rise condominium, and it was there that Steven for the first time in his life saw firsthand how the "other half" lived: beautiful apartments, maids, luxury automobiles, parties with the rich and the famous. "Why not me?" he kept asking himself.

Along the lines of "When the student is ready, the mentor will arrive," in Steven Waldon's case he arrived not with the pot of gold but with the road map that would lead to it. Steven had always been good with his hands and had saved the family money by cutting their hair. One day, a successful friend of his father's stopped by and asked Steven to give him a trim. Steven did, and the businessman suggested that Steven not only seemed to enjoy the process but was actually good at it. He counseled Steven to study haircutting at Lakewood Beauty College, and a government grant allowed him to go back to school.

He attended classes during the day, worked at his security job all night, and slept and studied in the few hours in between. Talk about conation! After his graduation, we finally hired him at Visible Changes, and here, I think, is a good point to turn the narrative over to Steven:

"I started working in the back room shampooing from morning until night. It was like boot camp! My back was really hurting. I was the new kid back there, so I took advantage of getting to do more work with the idea that I would outsell all those other girls, even if they had been there longer. I wanted to beat them and I did. Once I got promoted out of the back room, my problems started.

"When your first client sits in your chair, you're petrified. You might as well be wearing a sign that says, Lack of Confidence, No Courage. They can read that look on your face. You get the feeling that the customer knows you just got out of the back room and that you don't know what you're doing. When that happens, you have to think about all the months of training that you've been through.

"I started off by doing a few bad cuts that had to be redone. In some cases, I didn't do exactly what the client asked for because I didn't know how. My main problem was this lack of confidence. I never realized how much confidence plays a role in your life's success.

"So I got sent back to the back room after three months on the floor for remedial work and training. I was really devastated when I had to go back to wearing the back-room T-shirt and give up the white shirt and smock that the haircutters wore. I was really bitter at first and, later, embarrassed and ashamed. I thought I was the only one ever to have to go through such a humiliation. At first, I blamed John and Maryanne.

Conation

"After a while, though, I started to ask myself the tough questions: Had I really given it my best? Had I really given 100 percent? I knew that I hadn't, so I gave myself a three-month probation period on the job. This time, I decided to really try.

"Then, I said to myself that I was going to do this the best I could, and, if I failed, I would never tell myself I had failed because I hadn't really tried. I didn't want that kind of an excuse.

"I began to really check my haircuts and finally, after a struggle, got back onto the floor, and this time I vowed to myself that I would never be intimidated again. THIS IS MY DOMAIN! I knew that no one could take this away from me unless I allowed it.

"I began to read cosmetology books, and I tried to treat my customers great. I wanted them to feel good about coming to see me, and I always tried to make it special for them. I really pampered every one of them.

"Finally, I began to hit my performance goals. The first time that I hit my goal, my manager made me feel like a king—big time." In fact, Steven's parents joined him at the salon when he was awarded, of all things, a cupcake for meeting his goals. Says Steven, "It's a little bit embarrassing to admit to people that a cupcake changed my life, but it really did. Talk about feeling proud!

"I began to model myself on other successful people: One woman sold a lot of retail and had a great attitude. I made it my goal to beat her in retail and the following year when I went onstage at our company conference to accept the top retail sales trophy, it was one of the proudest moments of my life. Another woman was a master cutter. She worked hard, gave excellent customer service, and her finish work was perfect. I really looked up to her. She had a taste of success, and I had a desire to be like her.

"A lot of the other young people in the salon didn't have that

Applying the Laws of Success

desire. I think it was because they had had it too easy in life—their parents gave them too much, or they had never worked hard at a real job. Believe me, until you have lifted pipe until you think your back is going to break, you haven't worked hard! I thought that if these people knew what real work was like, they would have thought that this was a breeze. The heaviest things we pick up are the bottles of products!

"I knew that I had several handicaps—being black, being male. A lot of people stereotype male hairdressers as being gay, and some clients don't want males or gays to work on them. But I told myself I could no longer worry about those things I couldn't change. To be fair to myself, I either had to quit or give it my best shot. I chose to give it my best shot.

"I don't think negative thoughts anymore, and I always analyze everything that I think about. That is what determines my mood. I can't function when I'm unhappy. I have begun to listen to some of the motivational tapes that John recommends, and I now constantly read motivational and self-help books. If you feed your mind enough good things, you stop listening to people who have given up on themselves and life.

"I know that I have more confidence now—in a good sense—because, for example, when I used to walk around the mall and come eye to eye with someone, I used to always look down. I got sick of that. I hate it when I do that. I always thought about it and asked myself, WHY????? I still do it occasionally.

"I now know that I don't have to do that. Now I walk in the mall and I look at people and smile. I know practically everybody in the mall. I call them all by their names. I ask them how they are, and I really care. I acknowledge them. They reward me by caring back. I'm sincere—and so are they.

"If you don't like what you're doing, you must change it or get an education, so you don't have to accept what people give you.

Conation

You are in control. I think about that commercial that says, 'A mind is a terrible thing to waste.' That is so true. Now, my clients see me as a haircutter that really knows his business. I don't just want to cut hair. I want to use all this input I've gotten over the years. I am now going out to classes and giving motivational talks, which I never could have done before. I know now that you have to prove yourself. It's not enough just to tell someone that you can do something or that you are a hard worker—you have to do it and be it.

"If you show that you are willing to try, people will help you. A lot of my clients love me. I have everything in place now. I sold $29,000 in retail last year and was tops in my salon. I now feel that no one will ever beat me in that salon. Last year my total volume was $91,000. This year I am going for $110,000. My retail goal is $33,000. Last year I made $3,700 in bonuses, and more than $30,000 in all. This is the most that I have ever accomplished. I have a new Suzuki Samurai and my own apartment with really nice furniture. I never realized that I would ever be able to live like this.

"I'll let you in on a secret: it's who you hang out with that makes the difference. Until you are around people who are successful, or striving to be successful, you most likely won't be successful yourself. I can now be around negative people and still keep my mind set on what I want, but I couldn't always do that. Today I punch all that negative out of them. It's like they can't change me because it's solid in me. I've seen what it's like and how it feels. It's not that I look down on them, but I'm proud of what I've accomplished. I tell them that you have to do everything as well as you can. You have to take responsibility for yourself and make sure that you give 100 percent. You can't blame things on other people, and even though you can't please everyone, you can come pretty close. I know that I feel good if I give 100 percent.

Applying the Laws of Success

"Is there still a lot of prejudice against blacks? No, I don't think so, but I'm not sure that I would recognize it because my attitude is so different now. It's like I know that I can win people over and compete on anybody's terms. Life has so much to offer, regardless of your color, if you only take advantage of it."

I think a fitting closing to this chapter is a quotation from Jon Erickson that describes the mind-set of all people with their fair share of conation. It reads:

"I found that I could find the energy . . . that I could find the determination to keep on going. I learned that your mind can amaze your body, if you just keep telling yourself, I can do it . . . I can do it . . . I can do it!"

Action Plan

- **It's true that tough times come for everyone, but it's also true that the source of most tough times is lack of direction.**

When Tony Hatty had forty or fifty jobs during school, is it any wonder he didn't get anywhere? Once he had a single goal—to become the top producer (in both haircutting and retail sales) at Visible Changes—his conation took over and he was unstoppable. Remember, a 100 percent commitment to one goal is more than twice as good as a 50 percent commitment to two goals. The difference between doing and dabbling is focus.

- **If you're black or yellow, like Steven or Le, you're never going to overcome the prejudice by being "just as good" as everyone else out there.**

You've got to be better. It's not fair, but it's fact.

Conation

- **Don't look down.**

Rather than lowering your eyes next time a stranger approaches you, try this: look him or her squarely in the eyes, smile, and say "Hi." When McDonald's was preparing to open its first outlet in Moscow, the most difficult task for trainers was teaching their employees to smile—things had been grim for so long in the Soviet Union. Sounds simple, doesn't it? Success by smiling, but it works and it's infectious.

- **As Le Van Vu demonstrated, being born into wealth or even acquiring great wealth does not ensure lasting wealth.**

It's the drive to come back, that is, conation, that guarantees a return to success after any misstep or misfortune.

- **Conation, although we don't totally understand it, can be nurtured in later life.**

In the next chapter, we'll see that people who lack conation need more motivation. Once motivation becomes internalized and automatic, it turns into conation, which is permanent.

Chapter 6

Motivation

BECAUSE OF THE incredible productivity of our staff at Visible Changes, I am often asked to give talks and seminars on motivation, as if I possessed some great secret that somehow has escaped the seven-figure-income executives at IBM or most of the other Fortune 500 companies.

Our customers tell us that, in addition to walking into one of our salons and out again with a great haircut, one of the things they enjoy most about the Visible Changes experience is what could be called the "Four E's": the **excitement,** the **enthusiasm,** the **energy,** and the **electricity** evident in every one of our locations. Our staff not only appear to be happy, they *are* happy. Their smiles are real, and their positive mind-set is genuine.

And, of course, there is no more infectious or contagious attitude than enthusiasm. It's probably the most undervalued asset in any corporation, and yet most managers pay little, if any, attention to it.

Remember, while Henry David Thoreau wrote that "most men lead lives of quiet desperation," it was his best friend, Ralph Waldo Emerson, who wrote, "Nothing great was ever achieved without enthusiasm." People want to be around other people who are passionate about what they do. If you'll allow me one more quotation from the master-motivator of all time. Vince Lombardi: "If you are not fired up with enthusiasm, you'll be fired with enthusiasm!"

And that, quite frankly, is the other side—and probably the most important side—of motivation. As super-motivator Anthony Robbins has pointed out, "It is associating pain, discomfort, or negative consequences with not performing, that results in making positive changes in one's behavior." I'd like to tell you that people are motivated more by the carrot than by the stick, but my experience tells me otherwise. The way to really get many people moving, including myself, is to associate pain with not acting and pleasure with achieving desired results. In most cases, but certainly not all, the emphasis unfortunately has to be on the pain. When a person can no longer bear being overweight, for example, he or she goes on a diet or exercise program. When the weight becomes so unbearable or unpleasant, the scales tip from wishing to acting.

Let me share a real-life story with you. A friend of mine had recently started a business and had high hopes of running it more or less along the lines of a participatory democracy. The structure was to be horizontal (We're all equals), rather than vertical (I'm on top of you), and decisions were to be made after discussion took place and consensus was reached.

After about three months into this venture, however, my friend began to notice that more and more of his employees were straggling in later and later, so of course he convened a meeting to attempt to discover what was wrong. He explained that everyone needed to be in at the appointed hour because that's when potential clients were most accessible, and that the future of the company, as well as of the individuals in the company, depended on the collective performance of the team.

Everyone was heard from. No one disagreed. Everyone pledged to report to work on time from that point on. And they did. For about a week, until the pattern began to repeat itself, and of course my friend called another meeting.

"Listen," he told them, "this is getting serious, and it really can't go on. We're falling farther and farther behind, and a new company cannot afford this kind of performance. We all need to be in here by nine." Again, there was general agreement, total commitment, and great performance—for about another week, until things again began to slide.

Motivation

At the outset of the third meeting, my friend took a different approach: "Anyone," he said, "who is not in here by 9 A.M. from now on is fired. Period. No discussion. This meeting is adjourned."

At last report, no one had been fired, because no one had been late.

Admittedly, this is a harsh example, but there must be downside consequences to continued bad behavior.

What my friend did, pure and simple, was attach real consequences to bad behavior, and what was the result? The behavior changed.

Let's go back to our overweight friend who is tempted to eat a large piece of chocolate cake. The decision-making process probably will go something like this: "I know I shouldn't eat this cake, but I'm already so fat, so what difference will one more piece of cake make?" Gulp! Maybe just one more sliver.

What this cake eater needs to do is increase the amount of pain associated with eating the cake—enough to outweigh the momentary pleasure that the cake eating will give him or her. To change behavior, the thought process needs to be, "If I eat this cake, I'll continue a pattern that is taking years off my life, ruining my personal relationships, causing people to laugh at me, making havoc of my social life, probably costing me promotions in my job, making me feel lousy all the time about myself, and, overall, making my life totally miserable. On the other hand, when I was thin, I was attractive, energetic, confident, happy, and popular."

That is the real equation. Do you think in the latter case the person would eat the cake? Probably not. To repeat, to motivate anyone, including yourself, associate pain, consequences, and negativity with not changing, and associate pleasure, esteem, and benefits with making the desirable changes.

No one was better at this technique than Vince Lombardi. The tougher he was with his men, the more they loved him, and the more they won on Sunday afternoons, the more they loved themselves. Let me take a moment to pay homage to one of my heroes and his phenomenal record:

In the nine years Lombardi was with the Green Bay Packers, he won 141 games, lost 39, and tied 6. For fourteen consecutive years before the arrival of Lombardi, the Packers had never had a winning season! For the three years previous to his arrival, they won only one game each season. The team was so bad that the hometowners would actually boo the players when they spotted them on the street.

In his introductory address to his players, Lombardi told them that they had never been part of a winning team and he had never been part of a losing team and, therefore, he was in charge, and they were going to do things his way. The record speaks for itself:

- First Year: Preseason, 4 wins, 2 losses; regular season, 7 wins, 5 losses. Third in Western Division.
- Second Year: Preseason, 6 wins, no losses; regular season, 8 wins, 4 losses. Western Division champions.
- Third Year: Preseason, 5 wins, no losses; regular season, 11 wins, 3 losses. Western Division champions.
- Fourth Year: Preseason, 6 wins, no losses; regular season, 13 wins, 1 loss. NFL champions.
- Fifth Year: Preseason, 5 wins, 1 loss; regular season, 11 wins, 2 losses. Second in Western Division.
- Sixth Year: Preseason, 3 wins, 2 losses; regular season, 8 wins, 5 losses, 1 tie. Second in Western Division.
- Seventh Year: Preseason, 4 wins, 1 loss; regular season, 10 wins, 3 losses, 1 tie. NFL champions.
- Eighth Year: Preseason, 3 wins, 2 losses; regular season, 12 wins, 2 losses. NFL champions.
- Ninth Year: Preseason, 6 wins, no losses; regular season, 9 wins, 4 losses, 1 tie. NFL champions.

Motivation

This is essentially the same team that hadn't had a winning season in fourteen years before it met Lombardi! Now, I ask, shouldn't this guy be studied in every classroom in America? He wasn't teaching football, he was teaching life. Lombardi knew that if you wanted something in life, you had to plan for it, prepare yourself for it, and then, most important, you had to go for it.

There is an old saying that "a thousand wishes won't fill a bucket with fishes." Instead, it takes some fishing, and some getting up early in the morning, and some self-discipline, and a fundamental belief that it's possible to catch some fish.

A misconception about "taking action" is that thinking, feeling, or talking about something long enough will lead to the "impulse" that will lead to action or forward motion. In other words, if I think about something long enough, eventually I'll get inspired enough to do it.

Unfortunately, it doesn't work that way. In fact, it's exactly the opposite. Thinking and feeling do not produce action. Action produces thinking and feeling. Once action has begun, it takes over and becomes unconscious, and this leads to an almost higher state of consciousness. Psychologist Abraham Maslow called these results "peak experiences" and others have called the phenomenon simply "flow." Mark Twain put it another way: "Thunder is good; thunder is impressive; but it is the lightning that gets the job done."

We all have experienced those times when we feel terrific, all-powerful and all-confident, and totally "in the moment." The way to achieve this wonderful feeling, thankfully, is quite simple: We simply have to overcome the inertia in which we usually reside, make the initial effort to accomplish any task . . . and that's all. Our bodies and our minds will take it from there. Remember, moving is actually easier than standing still.

One of the difficulties we encounter at Visible Changes with new staff is just getting them "up to the starting line." They've been told from Day One that they'll never amount to anything, and they've been fulfilling that prophecy ever since.

One of Houston's wise men, family counselor John Bradshaw, tells a story about how once in a while he'll come home from the office feeling down, dejected, or depressed. He'll unlock the front door to his house and his hound dog will be so happy to see him that he'll bark, squeal, jump up and down, and run around in circles. That makes Bradshaw feel good.

So Bradshaw will walk right through the house and out the back door, around the house, and reenter through the front door. And, of course, the dog will repeat the same welcoming ceremony, slobbering all over him as if he hasn't seen his master for months.

It raises that philosophical question, "Which would you rather be, unhappy like Aristotle or contented like a pig?" For better or worse, humans are the only living organisms both blessed and cursed with reflective memory. If we as children were told we were worthless and incapable of accomplishing great deeds, those are the messages we continually reflect upon and replay to ourselves literally hundreds of times each day. If that weren't bad enough, these messages are embedded so deeply in our subconscious that we rarely realize we are listening to such a continuing chorus of negativity.

At Visible Changes, we supply our people with a different set of tapes. We constantly praise and reward our people in recognition of their accomplishments, and, whenever possible, we do so in public. In effect, we are replacing negative "tapes" with positive ones.

Citing Maslow again, he once asked the class he was teaching at Brandeis University who among the students expected to accomplish great things in life. No hands went up. Maslow retorted, "Well, if not you, then who?"

If you want to see perfect examples of motivation and enthusiasm, just watch children for a while. As we worked on this chapter,

Motivation

my five-year-old son came bounding into my study, prattling on about one thing or another. I told him that his daddy was working and couldn't play with him at the moment. That brought a response of first, anger, and second, tears. I then told him that in about an hour, I would go swimming with him and we could do laps in our pool. He ran out of the room, squealing with delight.

Of course, he had associated swimming with fun because his experiences in the pool have been fun. Just because we're adults doesn't mean that we won't work better, harder, and with more excitement and enthusiasm if we genuinely enjoy our work and have fun doing it. Why this fundamental fact has escaped most managers, frankly, escapes me.

Unfortunately, enthusiasm is not the only attitude that can spread throughout an organization. Emotional viruses, such as gloom, doom, despair, and just plain laziness, can infect an institution and not only cripple it but actually kill it. As a manager, I have to stay on top of this every day.

To get to our salon in Houston at the Northwest Mall, most of our customers have to pass a competitor along the way. I always make it a point to check out the competition, and invariably, the place is empty, the floors are dirty, the haircutters are slouched down in chairs, usually smoking cigarettes and joking among themselves. They'll be out of business twelve months from now, no doubt about it.

Why, then, it makes sense to ask, have American businesses failed so miserably in motivating their work forces and in establishing a sense of excitement among their workers? Walk into any K mart (as opposed to a Wal-Mart), or, even better still, any post office, on a Friday afternoon and try to get even a smile out of an employee. Talk about low care-level!

During labor negotiations between General Motors and its key union, the United Auto Workers, a reporter asked an assembly-line worker whether he would be in favor of linking increased productivity to increased benefits. The worker responded, "Hell, you think I'm going to bust my butt for General Motors? I don't even bust my butt for myself!"

"Remember," said W. C. Fields, "a dead fish can float downstream, but it takes a live one to swim upstream." Just think of how many "floaters" are now in place at every level in American business.

My short course to turn "floaters" into swimmers follows:

- First, you must commit yourself to your enterprise and its objectives. If you're not excited about what you're doing, it's a sure bet that your employees aren't going to be excited either. Remember, enthusiasm spreads from the top down.
- Second, you must let your employees know through your every action, deed, and conversation that they are the most important assets in your organization, that they matter, that they are worthwhile. I stay up half the night sometimes, thinking of new ways to recognize and reward the staff of Visible Changes.

  Contrary to the current wisdom, I always put my staff even ahead of my customers. If you take care of your staff, your staff will take care of your customers.
- Third, let your people know that not only do *they* matter, but *what they do* matters. It is impossible to be motivated unless you believe that what you're doing has meaning and importance. Not having something to feel important about in life, for me, would be a pretty good definition of hell.

An old folk tale says it best:

Three men are doing the same job on a construction site when a passerby approaches and asks each man the same question: What are you doing?

Motivation

   The first laborer replies, "Are you blind? I'm lifting these rocks."

   The second employee answers, "I'm just a poor man who toils from dawn to dusk. I'm earning a living."

   The third worker responds with excitement and animation, "I'm building a cathedral."

Which of these three men do you believe gets out of bed in the morning, looks forward to the new day, and works with vigor and fervor in the carrying out of his daily labor?

At Visible Changes, *my* grander purpose, simply put, is to provide the opportunity to hundreds of our staff to lead better, happier, more productive, and more fulfilling lives. It's what keeps me up late at night and what keeps me getting up early in the morning. I once asked Ray Kroc, the founder of McDonald's, what he was most proud of in his career, and he answered without a pause, "McDonald's has been able to help create more millionaires in this country than any other corporation in the history of the world."

Maryanne's purpose is to upgrade her profession and, as a result, change the image of an entire industry. It is a noble and uplifting goal, and every member at Visible Changes is engaged in accomplishing it.

Ask yourself the question, How can you have a well-run company if your staff don't think that their jobs are important? The fact is, every job is important. Sam Walton, one of the richest people in America, knows this intuitively. Recently one of his Wal-Marts in Florida was planning to put on a concert of some sort in the parking lot over the weekend, and ol' Sam decided to fly down, unannounced, and have a look for himself.

He arrived on a Friday, walked into one of his stores, and found himself in the middle of a crisis: an electrical storm had knocked out his electronic cash registers, and the lines were getting longer and longer at the checkout counters. What did Sam do (and I remind you, he's in his seventies)? He got out his pad and pencil and started working his way through the lines, toting up the purchases for his patrons, rounding off the "cents" (downward) on the price tags so he could work faster.

Do you think his checkout clerks have held their heads a little bit higher since that day?

Once you start looking down on your staff, you're headed for trouble. One of the great problems in large corporations is that the top echelons are separated from the people who actually do the work. They park in executive parking lots, eat in executive dining rooms, freshen up in executive restrooms, and take huge salaries and bonuses regardless of how the company is performing.

When entrepreneur H. Ross Perot became the largest shareholder in General Motors, he was struck by the fact that the company was losing hundreds upon hundreds of millions of dollars, while the top executives continued to reward themselves with multimillion-dollar bonuses.

Then, when labor negotiations rolled around, management took the bargaining position of, "No raises this year, guys. We're losing money. We're broke."

Does top GM management think its employees are stupid? Yes, it does. Are its employees stupid? No, they're not.

But let's get back to some of the more specific things we do at Visible Changes to keep our motivation level high.

From the very beginning, Maryanne and I would visit each salon on Saturday mornings to share with our managers and all of our staff how we were doing as a company, what our plans were, and to listen to what each and every one of them had to say. We'd always bring an audiotape by a great motivational speaker, such as Zig Ziglar or Napoleon Hill, and we'd listen to these tapes together.

Motivation

I still spend thousands of dollars each year on motivational tapes, books, and live speakers, and many of our staff listen to them constantly, often while driving to and from work in the terrible Houston traffic. Do motivational tapes work? There is no question that they work.

Also, it may sound like a little thing, but Maryanne calls each and every staff member on each and every birthday and employment anniversary to share with them greetings, good wishes, and thanks. Does this sound like just a gesture? Yes. Are gestures important in companies? Yes again.

Twice a year, each staff member spends one-on-one time with either Maryanne or me. During these talks, we listen, we learn, and we share our goals and dreams with our people. We also review the staff member's performance over the last six months and set performance goals for the future. We also give out bonuses and superbonuses, and one of the great pleasures of my life is to hand out large rewards for superior work. Conversely, like any parent, I would prefer to reward, rather than punish or admonish, but there are those times when some staff, for whatever reason, simply are slacking off, and we always face these situations head on.

More often than not, it is our staff themselves who take it upon themselves to work with or, let's face it, get rid of others who simply aren't doing their jobs. Each of our sixteen salons each year competes among the others for hundreds of thousands of dollars' worth of bonuses, trips, automobiles, and other prizes, so every staff member is expected by the others to be part of the team and to do his or her part.

At our corporate headquarters, our walls are filled with plaques, which in turn are filled with names of our people who have achieved their personal performance goals. We always reward and pat our people on the back in full view of the widest possible audience. In many cases, this recognition is the only public applause they have ever received.

Over the years, our staff have continually set higher and higher performance standards for themselves—and they've always surpassed them.

In addition to our one-on-one meetings, Maryanne and I gather all of our people together at our corporate offices four times a year. Because of our incredible growth in people—and limited growth in meeting space—these quarterly meetings take us about a week, since we can cram only about a hundred people into our largest meeting room.

These sessions are especially important for morale and motivation in our company, because they give us an opportunity to challenge our people to reach even greater heights. When I address them, I promise you, I'm not a cheerleader. I don't tell them how great everything is. My job is to make them think about such questions as:

How are we going to renew? What are we going to do if we're no longer No. 1? Why are some of our three- or four-year people now outselling some of our ten-year people? Is our training everything it should be?

But I also go far beyond just business concerns and opportunities. I might get into anything from opportunities to buy a home while the market is low to the need to spend quality time with children.

It is also at these quarterly meetings that we ask each staff member to vote on whether Maryanne and I stay or go as heads of Visible Changes. The staff know what our sales are, they know what our salaries are, and they get to vote by blind ballot on whether they want us to continue to run the company.

Such a vote, I promise you, puts us a lot more on the hot seat than, say, a proxy vote of the shareholders of a large corporation.

Motivation

In most cases, shareholders, or even directors, have no idea how well their top executives are performing. Can you imagine the management of Sears allowing their employees to determine whether or not they get to keep their jobs? Believe me, if they did, there would be a lot more accountability in those corporations, and the companies would be run a lot better. You can fool a lot of people in business, but you can't fool the people you work with. The relationship is too close.

Over the years, however, our quarterly meetings have gotten more and more difficult to do, since in effect we give the same presentation at each of five successive all-day sessions, and both Maryanne and I have to be "on" without a break.

Nevertheless, their positives far outweigh their negatives, and we believe they are just one more way of staying in touch with our people and letting them know what's going on in *their* company.

P.S.: So far the votes have been overwhelmingly in our favor—but they haven't been unanimous.

The most grand, and most expensive, company get-together is something we call the "company conference." In effect, it's a gala party for our hundreds of employees, and we generally spend about a half-million dollars on the one-night affair.

The entire evening takes on the atmosphere of an inaugural ball with a little bit of *Wheel of Fortune* mixed in. I'm the master of ceremonies, and, in addition to the dining and the dancing, Maryanne and I give out our company awards and our individual awards for excellence. It's very much along the lines of, "Will you pass the envelope, please?"

All in all, last year we handed out nearly $150,000 in bonuses and individually recognized nearly 350 of our staff members and managers for their achievements. One by one, we invited them to join us onstage to receive their bonus and prizes. We gave away three new Datsun ZX's and announced that we were taking our

Applying the Laws of Success

sixty top performers on a week-long, expense-paid trip to Hawaii. Evenings such as this bring us together as a company and foster the enthusiasm and excitement among our staff that result in our success.

Is a half-million dollars a lot to spend on a one-night party? Definitely. Is it worth every penny? Definitely. Is there a company in the country that is doing $10 million a year in sales that can't afford to give away a couple of cars to staff who are their top achievers? Definitely not.

The author F. Scott Fitzgerald used to say that he liked to host parties that "changed people's lives." At Visible Changes, we like to throw parties that literally change the way our staff think about their work, about their company, and, most important, about themselves.

Action Plan

- **Motivation can be either positive or negative.**

("I want to go there" vs. "I want to get out of here".) For almost all of us, at the beginning of our journey negative motivations are the most effective. When our negatives get too bad, we finally are forced to react positively to change them. I wish I could tell you that adversity and being miserable are not important ingredients to success, but they are. They give you the "I ain't ever goin' back there attitude," and that attitude is very tough to beat when the chips are down.

- **Commitment to a meaningful purpose or goal is the most important ingredient in motivation.**

Commitment is the internal engine that drives you forward each day, heading in a direction that is important to you. Commitment adds the meaning to life.

Motivation

- **If commitment is the engine, public recognition is the fuel.**

Regardless of our success or station in life, we all need the approbation and applause of people important to us. If you're a manager, and you're going to praise a staff member for a job well done, find a way to do it in public. It will have at least a tenfold effect.

- **To build any cathedral requires at least one person with a higher purpose.**

Nearly every great company has had this individual at its helm during its formative years.

- **People in authority must make themselves available to the staff so the staff know that they are really no different and that they can ascend to the same heights you did.**

This "management by walking around," as it's called, is integral to the way we operate at Visible Changes.

- **The most important asset any company has is not its patents, bricks, mortar, buildings, or bank accounts but its people.**

From the janitor to the president, everyone must be taught to dream, to believe, and to accomplish.

- **Distinguish between "interest" and "commitment."**

The difference is critical, since "interest" almost never leads to results, whereas "commitment" always does. On any project, "interested" people go by the wayside; "committed" people go to the finish line.

Part Three

The Tools:
Don't Leave Home
without Them

Chapter 7

Education

ANYONE WHO BELIEVES that business and public education are not as connected as Siamese twins, with the very well-being of the one depending on the heartbeat of the other, hasn't been reading the local papers. It's like that line from Nietzsche: "He who smiles has not yet heard the bad news." And in the case of public education, the news is very bad indeed.

In fact, in the Houston Independent School District, from which we draw most of our applicants for Visible Changes, the news is so bad and the bureaucracy so entrenched that I decided I had to start my own school. It's called Visible Changes University, or "VCU" for short, and it opened its doors in the spring of 1990.

The main difference is that only about half of our curriculum deals with vocational training: cutting hair, doing perms, applying makeup, etc. The other half is dedicated to teaching life skills: balancing a checkbook, getting a loan from a bank, running a computer, increasing one's self-esteem. As I write these words, we are putting into place an extensive reading, writing, and oral presentation program, since most of our students and staff never gained these essential skills during their twelve years in public education.

We begin with such basics as customer relations—how to talk to customers, how to carry on a conversation. We make sure they read the newspaper every day, especially the front page, the business section, the sports section, and the fashion and life-style sections. It's an easy, straightforward way to have something to talk about to any customer and not come across as a dummy.

As important as what we encourage them to talk about are the things we don't want them talking about: their boyfriends or girlfriends, their sex lives, their fantasies, or the parties they went to the previous weekend.

The Tools: Don't Leave Home without Them

We counsel them on what to wear and how to wear their own hair. We don't want anyone looking like freaks at VCU or at Visible Changes. No purple hair on the heads of our haircutters!

Although VCU is a "beauty school," physically as well as academically it is unlike any other vocational school in the country. First of all, VCU is big, and second, it's beautiful. An average cosmetology school in America might cram 300 students into less than 5,000 square feet. Ours is 22,000 square feet and can accommodate 450 to 500 students. Everything in the school, from the marble in the restrooms to the latest audio and video technology, was put into place with one goal in mind: to increase the self-esteem of our students—and of our staff.

We wanted to give them a facility they could be proud of, a place they'd want to show off to their friends and relatives, a place probably better than they've ever been in or worked in before. Money, I must tell you, was never a consideration. In fact, on a ledger sheet, this project doesn't make any sense. We invested a couple million dollars in the school, which won't make a nickel's profit for at least five years—if ever.

What did make sense to us, however—in fact, what was crystal-clear—was that if we couldn't get good applicants to come to work at Visible Changes, in effect we were going to be out of business. We looked at VCU as a cost of doing business for Visible Changes, and I challenge other businesses to look into setting up in-house schools to repair the damage being done by our public schools.

In dollar terms alone, American industry this year will spend $80 billion, that's billion with a *b*, on remedial education. Listen to Louis V. Gerstner, Jr., chairman and CEO of RJR Nabisco, addressing a group of business executives in Houston.

"Where am I going to get the competent people RJR Nabisco will need in the future?

"As my current labor force retires, where will I find the young people I need to replace them? . . .

Education

"My company is not organized to teach a high school graduate how to read. But that is what I, and every corporate chief executive in America, must face today—an annual crop of entrants to the labor force that every year contains a higher proportion of functional illiterates.

"The results of this educational drought go straight to the bottom line—lost customers, poor product quality, lost shipments, garbled paperwork. Do I have to continue this list?"

Let me tell you what inspired me to start my own school.

At a quarterly meeting of the staff of Visible Changes, I went before the group and asked what seemed to be an innocuous, off-the-cuff question:

"How many of you would want your children to receive the same-quality education you received going through the public school system?" Out of our five hundred or so people, one hand went up—and that young man was educated in Taiwan.

Consider this analogy, raised in the *New York Times* by Albert Shanker, president of the American Federation of Teachers:

What would the president of IBM do if 25 percent of all his computers fell off the conveyor belt before they reached the end of the line, and of those 75 percent that did make it to the end, 90 percent of them were in need of serious remedial repair? This is exactly what is happening in our public schools.

But in fact, America's schools are producing something far more dangerous than defective computers. They are producing defective children, and the social and monetary costs to this country are becoming unbearable. The numbers are staggering:

Nearly 27 million Americans are now functionally illiterate. They cannot read a bus schedule or the warning label on a prescription bottle of medicine. Nearly 600,000 high school seniors who are graduating this year will not be able to read the writing on their own diplomas. And they have been in school six hours a day for twelve years! What on earth have they been doing for twelve years?

The Tools: Don't Leave Home without Them

But if the economic costs of our public school system are enormous—and they are—the social costs are even more staggering. Lack of education and knowledge is the root of nearly every social problem America faces today.

In recent years, public education has largely gone the route of public housing: a refuge of last resort for those too poor, too powerless, or too disenfranchised to break out of, or improve, the system. Anyone who knows enough and can afford to pull their children out of this educational morass does so.

The reason I've gotten so interested in public education is that in large measure, I feel as though I was a victim of that same system, even though I went through it some twenty-five years ago. It was bad then and has gotten steadily worse since.

I snored through most of my classes, and I was as glad to get out of high school as the principal was to see me go. The quality of both of our lives, I'm sure, improved immediately and immeasurably.

I got my real education on the streets and on my own. And maybe it's because I feel the public education system let me down that I'm now such a crusader to fix it. But even more important, I believe that many of the techniques we employ at Visible Changes are directly relevant to turning around our nation's schools.

After all, our labor pool is made up primarily of people like myself, whom the public schools had largely written off as losers. In fact, the above-cited Shanker once wrote a marvelous column about the "bottom halfers," that is, the students in the bottom half of the class who went on to accomplish far greater deeds than the elite at the top.

(I have a friend here in Houston who, like me, was born a poor boy, did only so-so in school, and went on to build a business empire worth several hundred million dollars. Remembering his

Education

struggle with the books, he later set up a scholarship at the University of Texas for "C" students and below!)

At VCU, we're lining the halls with pictures of phenomenally successful people—the "late bloomers" in life whom the system had written off as losers. Albert Einstein was one. (While Einstein is known largely for his equation $E=MC^2$, he came up with another equation for success: "If A equals success, then the formula is A equals X plus Y plus Z, with X being work, Y play, and Z keeping your mouth shut.") We want our people to get the message that only they have the right to make the judgment on whether they are winners or losers, and, of course, we constantly encourage them to think of themselves as winners or, at the least, emerging winners.

At VCU, we are putting into place those intangibles that are more important to learning than dollar signs, and the reasons we know they will work are 1) they have worked for us at Visible Changes (and we have hundreds of success stories to prove it), and 2) they are just common sense.

Specifically at Visible Changes and at VCU, we concentrate on four essentials that have largely disappeared from the public school landscape but, if reintroduced, would go a long way toward reforming our public schools. I am talking about **standards, motivation, discipline,** and **accountability**—the very elements that my immigrant friends put to work to become successful in America—and the good news is that they don't cost one additional dime of taxpayer money. Education problems are largely problems of public will, not of the public purse.

In fact, public education is awash in money. It has become one of the largest growth industries in America, with huge corporations cranking out billions of dollars' worth of educational materials, textbooks, computer software, testing and evaluation services, and on and on.

The Tools: Don't Leave Home without Them

In 1989 alone, we spent more than $353 billion on our public schools! That's $50 billion more than on national defense and twice as much as Japan spent per pupil. And yet, in standardized math and science tests, American students scored dead-last in the industrialized world, coming in far behind Japan, Germany, Thailand, and Korea.

So costly has this tab become that in many state budgets, public education now accounts for half of all state expenditures, and with unbelievably abysmal results. And yet, the cry from the educational community, the very people who have presided over this disaster, is, in effect, "Send more money."

The National Education Association, headquartered just a few blocks from the White House, is the largest—and arguably the most powerful—labor union in the country, boasting 1.2 million members. That's a lot of teachers and administrators, but even more important from a politician's point of view, that's a lot of votes. In 1976, as a political payoff for NEA support in his election bid, President Jimmy Carter created a Washington behemoth called the Office of Education.

That Cabinet-level department now employs thousands of bureaucrats who spend much of their time driving local education officials crazy. They've been described as "ten thousand monkeys with ten thousand typewriters." Just as the Department of Energy has not produced one barrel of oil in this country, likewise the Office of Education has not produced one blip on any standardized test in America to suggest it is worth keeping in business. It is a perfect example of business consultant Peter Drucker's observation that "so much of what we call management consists of making it difficult for people to work!"

Let's examine the four principles I mentioned above and how they have eroded or disappeared from our schools:

Standards   In the last twenty years, we have steadily lowered academic standards to accommodate those whom we assumed,

Education

largely because of race or family background, could not be expected to achieve in school. We have inundated our classrooms with federal and state programs to compensate for the low expectations we have for children who come to school each morning from troubled homes.

The lesson we have inadvertently taught these children is that they are incapable of learning or accomplishing great things. We have created an underclass, not just economically but educationally.

At Visible Changes and at VCU, we follow the advice of Charles E. Wilson, former CEO of General Motors: "A good boss is one who makes people think they have more ability than they have, so they consistently do better work than they thought they could."

We let our people know from Day One that we expect great performances from them and that we will accept nothing less. Not surprisingly, most often we get it. Promotions and bonuses, we explain, are completely objective, so there is no favoritism, discrimination, or subjectivity. The computer keeps track of performance and progress toward individual and team goals, and, believe me, our computer system does not have a discriminatory or racist microchip in its body.

At Visible Changes, we don't believe there is anything genetic, behavioral, or social that dictates that our people can't get to work on time, work hard for eight hours a day, be happy, and do a great job—regardless of their race, history, or upbringing. While American business as a whole, thankfully, is in the process of raising its standards to compete internationally, the educational community continues to relax its performance standards. As the disparity grows wider, businesses, in their own enlightened self-interest, must step in to fill the gap. It's a classic question of "Pay me now or pay me later."

You've probably heard of the "dumbing down" of our text-

The Tools: Don't Leave Home without Them

books so even the most dim-witted can excel while the best and the brightest are bored to the point of dropping out or dozing off. As the British author G. K. Chesterton reminded us, "A yawn is a silent shout."

Even our teacher colleges and universities have lowered their standards in order to maintain their shrinking enrollments, and, as a consequence, they are now emptying an annual crop of thousands of underqualified teachers into the system. Today, an average high school graduate planning to become a teacher enters college with a combined SAT score of 855, a full 49 points lower than students entering college as a whole.

In New Orleans, a teacher with a master's degree sent the following note home to a parent:

"Johnie have a pom to rite and he fell to du it." A master's degree!

Please don't misunderstand my coming down hard on teachers, the universities that educate them, the unions that represent them, and the administrators who orchestrate the whole system. I'm only saying that until we set and enforce stringent standards on who can become—and who can remain—a teacher in our public schools, the American public will continue to hold the entire profession in low esteem. Pay increases will be given only grudgingly, and the best teachers will continue to leave the profession for careers that offer both more dignity and more pay.

Do we need to pay our teachers more? Yes, we do—in fact, much more—but only if salary increases are linked to demonstrated competence in the classroom. School boards should not consider across-the-board pay raises for teachers. In fact, bad teachers (and their colleagues know exactly who they are) need to be retrained, retired, or fired. Last year, out of a teacher population of nearly eleven thousand in Houston, only three were fired for incompetence. The year before, only two were fired. In Hous-

Education

ton, it takes, on average, three years to dismiss an incompetent teacher and costs the school district approximately ninety thousand dollars to work its way through the appeal process.

Is it any wonder why businesses need to take the matter into their own hands?

Let's return to our example of the 600,000 students who will graduate this year and not be able to read their own diplomas, since a few of them will apply to me for jobs. Have you ever wondered how this could happen? I did, I decided to look into it, and I found out. Here's how:

There is a concept, which is rampant in public schools across America, called "social promotion." The theory presumes that it is better to promote a failing student than to hold him or her back and risk damaging his or her "self-esteem."

And so, year after year, students who haven't the foggiest idea of what is going on in front of the classroom are being pushed through the system and, ultimately, out the front door twelve years later with a meaningless diploma in hand.

The reality, of course, is that those students who have been socially promoted devalue the diploma of every other student who will ever receive one from that institution. To paraphrase author George Orwell, it is an idea so absurd that only an educated mind would consider it. After twenty years of this nonsense, it seems fair to ask our professional educators, Where is the students' self-esteem now that they can't read, write, or get a decent job?

Motivation Although we devote an entire chapter in this book to motivation, let me be more specific here and suggest some ways that the techniques we have employed at Visible Changes might work equally well in our schools.

Reward without recognition, I've learned, is almost meaningless. I can stick an extra hundred bucks into somebody's pay envelope, and it means almost nothing to the staff member, to

The Tools: Don't Leave Home without Them

me, or to the company. On the other hand, if I call that person up publicly before her friends and peers, pat her on the back, and tell those assembled what a marvelous job she did—and by the way, here is a little token of our appreciation—that person experiences a feeling that all the financial rewards in the world couldn't match.

Who among us does not remember as a youngster being singled out for some special recognition in front of a class or perhaps at an athletic awards banquet? It might have been something as simple as having an excellent test paper posted on a bulletin board or our name published in the student newspaper for making the honor roll. It's that kind of public recognition that changes people's lives.

Therefore, at VCU, we recognize our students publicly for their accomplishments at every possible opportunity. Good grades are posted in public. Every attempt at improvement gets a public pat on the back. (We follow the lead of one large company in the Midwest that gives out daily "Atta-Boy Awards." Each day the manager posts in public a list of people who had done not necessarily great things, but good things, positive things for their clients or their customers. "Atta-boy, atta-way to go," they're told publicly.)

There is a Chinese proverb that says that all you have to do to beat a man down is to tell him ten times a day that he's worthless. He'll do the rest himself. I believe that the opposite is also true. Tell people publicly and frequently when they are doing well, and they will do even better. It's simple, it's free, and it works.

Discipline The concept of discipline has almost disappeared from our public classrooms. The teachers themselves, in many cases, grew up without discipline, passed through universities that didn't require discipline, and now are ill equipped to model it, demand it, or teach it to their students.

Education

Somehow along the way—perhaps "Sesame Street" was responsible—the idea has crept into vogue that education has to be fun. If a lesson or assignment isn't either entertaining or amusing, it is assumed to be beyond the capacity of our children to absorb it.

Therefore, the "old-fashioned way" of teaching reading, writing, science, geography, mathematics, or whatever, has fallen into disrepute. Students, so the theory goes, must "experience" these concepts, rather than "learn" them through repetition and drill.

Admittedly, education works better when it is fun or entertaining, but, unfortunately, other than keeping the "meat on the seat" and the mind on the task, there does not seem to be any way to transfer the multiplication tables or the conjugation of irregular Latin verbs from the tablet to the brain. As author/psychiatrist Scott Peck wrote in the opening line of his book *The Road Less Traveled,* "Life is difficult."

At Visible Changes and at VCU, we are discipline fanatics. We drill, drill, drill, until the lesson or the behavior becomes unthinking or automatic—and then we drill some more. For some students or staff, it takes more drill or study than for others, but in the end, everyone who puts in the effort and the hours finally "gets it," and *then* it becomes fun, thoughtful, and creative. On discipline, we are total contrarians: The public perception is that "hard is bad." We believe that "hard is good."

Accountability   When everyone is accountable for everything, no one is ultimately accountable for anything. Ask a member of the education bureaucracy to account for the armies of illiterates pouring out of the halls of the academe, and, I promise you, the answer will be "society."

They will tell you about single-parent teenage mothers, about drunken fathers, about crack-addicted babies, about malnutrition, child abuse, latchkey children, and an array of other social

The Tools: Don't Leave Home without Them

woes. In other words, they will tell you, until we have more money for more programs to cure society's problems, we won't be able to improve the performance of our public schools.

Don't you believe it.

In the past two decades we have thrown billions of dollars at the education problem, and every time we added more money, we bought more illiteracy. I think we've lost sight of why we have public schools in the first place.

The purpose of public education, pure and simple, is to give our children the basic tools and skills to make their way in the world and lead a reasonably responsible and happy life. No more, no less.

It is not the school's job to teach kids how to dribble a basketball, toot a trombone, have safe sex, or just say no to drugs.

We had a terrible brouhaha in Texas two years ago when the legislature mandated what became known as the "no pass–no play" rule. The idea was that if a student failed a course, he or she couldn't play sports or partake in other extracurricular activities.

The uproar from parents was deafening. For the most part, they didn't seem to care if their kids couldn't read or write, but no football? No cheerleading? That was downright un-American, certainly un-Texan. Some say it cost the governor his re-election.

An Associated Press story recently ran in the Houston newspaper under the headline: TEACHER WHO FLUNKED STAR PLAYER TO STAY ON PROBATIONARY STATUS. In part, the story read:

DALLAS—The teacher who was transferred from Carter High School after a dispute over a grade he'd given a star football player will remain on probation, a Dallas school district panel decided.

Wilfred Bates, 57, was transferred from teaching math

Education

at Carter to an industrial arts post at Gaston Middle School after failing player Gary Edwards, who district officials said passed Bates' algebra course.

Edwards' academic eligibility was crucial to the Carter team, eventually the state 5A champion. If Edwards failed, the team would have had to forfeit games he played while having the deficient grade. . . .

Edwards, a University of Houston signee, was arrested June 22 [1989] and accused of robbing two video stores in a Dallas suburb.

Like success, educating children is simple but difficult. Talking about educating children is complex but easy. The fact is, in both success and education, the fundamentals work. Fads, gimmicks, and theories are expensive, do not work, never have worked, and never will work. Linus Wright, the former school superintendent for the city of Dallas and undersecretary of education under President Reagan, had it exactly right when he said, "Education is as simple as two people, a teacher and a pupil, sitting on a log and talking to each other."

If you believe as I do that accountability has left the system—that everyone has excuses and explanations but no solutions—let me propose something that is so simple it may sound like a new thought:

First and foremost, the students themselves are responsible for their own education. It is our responsibility, as citizens and taxpayers, to assure that students have the *opportunity* to learn in school, but there our responsibility ends.

Nowhere, in all the discussions I've ever heard about "Why Johnny Can't Read," have I ever heard it suggested that maybe part of the fault lies with Johnny himself. Is Johnny paying attention in class? Is Johnny doing his homework assignments? Is

The Tools: Don't Leave Home without Them

Johnny giving it his best effort? If Johnny is not, I promise you, all of the programs, all of the technology, and all of the dollars we pour into the system will not make one whit of difference.

At Visible Changes, we always place the responsibility and accountability at the lowest possible level. It is only at that level where problems can really be solved. Any parent who thinks George Bush or the federal government is going to get his kid off drugs has got to be crazy or on drugs himself. The farther you get from the problem itself, the less influence you have in solving it.

Moving up the ladder of accountability in the educational chain, after the student, of course, comes the teacher. Good teachers who achieve good results need to be rewarded, and those who don't need to be replaced.

At Visible Changes University, we choose only the best and the brightest among our people to teach our new recruits. We revere our best teachers, and we recognize and reward them accordingly. At VCU, we built our system from the teachers up, not from the administrators down. The teacher is the only one in the system who teaches and so, by definition, is the most important player in the game. In the public schools, it is exactly the opposite. The dollars and the status lie outside the classroom—in administration—and those ranks are swelling.

Last in the accountability chain is the principal.

In the best school systems, the principal has broad authority and responsibility for the performance of the school. He or she can hire and fire teachers, set academic and disciplinary standards, and be judged on the results the institution achieves. The principal is the highest on-site official in the education chain and needs to be given the status of the CEO of a company.

If the school performs, the principal is easily worth $100,000. If it doesn't, he or she should be sent packing. Give this person the tools and, most important, the authority to do the job, and

Education

then get out of the way and let him or her do it. Too often boards of education keep pulling up the plants to see how the roots are doing.

To sum up, the model we employ at Visible Changes and VCU mirrors the one I'm advocating for our public schools. Each student is responsible for his or her own work. Each teacher is responsible for seeing that the students have the training to excel at their job, and the school director (read "principal") is responsible for the overall performance of the institution.

Maryanne and I make certain that all of these people have everything they need to do their jobs, but then we get out of the way and let them perform in their own individual way. We hold them accountable for their results and nothing else, and they are rewarded and recognized accordingly.

In the final analysis, our school is really nothing without our people. Bricks and mortar, even as fancy as they might be at VCU, do not a school make. Our dream is that after all the snapshots are taken at all the graduation ceremonies, our students will go on to contribute something back to our industry and our society. We want the students to ask, "Without that school, where would I be today?" Then we will have contributed something to our society.

Action Plan

- **Don't write yourself off just because you're in the bottom half of the class.**

Remember, half of the class graduates in the bottom half, and many outperform those at the top. Above all, don't accept any labels that people pin on you, like "loser," or "no-good," or "dreamer." (The only difference between being a "dreamer" and a "goal-setter" is adding a deadline to the dream.) I tell my people, many of whom are castoffs from the educational system, "Are you going to believe some $20,000-a-year guidance counselor who tells you you're no good, or are you going to believe someone like myself, who's made millions, who says you are?"

- ● **Get all of the education you can, all of your life, and develop a daily habit of reading.**

International Paper Company once produced a series of advertisements entitled "Send Me a Man Who Reads," and the ads couldn't have been more pointed. You might not be what you eat, but you are what you read, so get on a reading program. It's the only way to stay current, and competitive, in your field. It will also broaden your life and make you a more interesting person.

- ● **Education must have standards, motivation, discipline, and accountability.**

Standards: No one should be allowed to go through twelve years of education without knowing how to read at least at the high school level and how to do simple math in their heads (times tables up to 12, adding, dividing, and subtracting).

Motivation: Children, regardless of economic status, should be rewarded for their success in education by knowing that they'll go on to college or a trade school that will give them the necessary tools that will enable them to enjoy a fruitful life.

Discipline: Both the principal and teacher need to be allowed to reprimand children in order to have total control in the classroom for the well-being of the entire class—not just for a few troublemakers.

Accountability: We should hold students responsible for themselves, teachers responsible for their classes, and principals responsible for their entire schools.

- ● **Do something for humanity: get involved in education for others.**

Lack of quality education is at the root of nearly all of our society's problems—the obvious ones, such as crime, unemployment, and

Education

welfare—and some not so obvious. Educated people tend to be healthier, less likely to smoke, more likely to put on their seat belts, make more money, and generally lead better, more responsible lives. In your community, take an active interest in public education, go to school board meetings, and insist on high standards in the classroom. Your rewards will be forthcoming.

Chapter 8

Basic Training

$\mathbf{T}$HERE ARE PEOPLE in Houston, mainly women, who will swear to you that I have personally cut their hair. I haven't, I wouldn't, I couldn't, they wouldn't want me to, and I never will.

It is true that, on occasion, I will visit a salon, stand behind a chair of one of our "style directors," and act as if I know what I'm doing. I might even gently primp a coiffure or two, introducing myself to customers while deftly redirecting any questions on style, fashion, or technique to the cutter who really knows what he or she is doing.

In fact, I have never picked up a pair of scissors with the intention to cut, shape, trim, or maim, and anyone who thinks that cutting hair is easy has never cut hair. That's one reason that after all these years in the business, I still don't understand fully why hairdressing is held in such low esteem as a profession. In Texas, as in most states, hairdressers must be licensed by the state, and that requires completing at least fifteen hundred hours of courses at an accredited beauty school. The program usually takes about a year, which is approximately half the time it takes to get an MBA at a University.

Maryanne has adopted as her personal mission the monumental task of improving both the image and the reality of hairdressers in America (they enjoy much higher status throughout Europe and most of the world), and the means by which she is going about this task is by directing all of the resources at our disposal at professionalizing the industry.

While our focus is, of course, on Visible Changes and the haircutting industry, our methodology, I think, is applicable to any business in the country. It's called training, and it's the secret to our success at Visible Changes. I don't think it's an exaggeration

The Tools: Don't Leave Home without Them

to say that our haircutters are the best-trained in the world. The result, of course, is that you cannot get a better haircut anywhere at any salon at any price.

Now I'm not saying that you can't find more luxurious settings where you're paying more for the ambience than you are for a haircutter's skills. In fact, knowing what I now know about haircutting and, in particular, the terrible training that most haircutters receive, I wouldn't bring either of my two cocker spaniels to most of what you would think of as the "exclusive salons." Most of these haircutters simply do not do enough volume to become really good at what they do—and most weren't trained properly in the first place. A busy haircutter at an average salon might do one thousand haircuts a year. Our average cutters do five times that many, and our top cutters do seventy-five hundred. There's nothing they haven't seen, and there's no problem in hair that they haven't solved literally hundreds and hundreds of times.

While our training is probably our biggest strength, at the outset it was our biggest problem.

Before we opened our first salon in the Greenspoint Mall, Maryanne and I went to the Astrodome—once described as the "Eighth Wonder of the World"—on the night of a Houston Oilers football game. Our purpose, however, was not to watch the game, but to check out the haircuts of the sixty-thousand-plus fans.

We walked up and down the aisles, looking and sometimes laughing out loud. Houston, Texas, appeared to be the home of the "do-it-at-home" haircut. The "bowl cut" was especially popular. (To this day, approximately half of all the haircuts in America are still done in the home!)

Maryanne was excited. With haircuts like these, she didn't see how we could miss. And so, it was with great anticipation that we placed our first advertisement for haircutters to staff our first salon at the Greenspoint Mall.

The first week, Maryanne interviewed more than three hun-

Basic Training

dred applicants—and hired six. From that day until this, I have never seen a longer parade of freaks, geeks, he's that would be she's (and vice versa), and just plain oddballs in every mode of dress you can imagine—and some you can't—than the group that wanted to work at the original Visible Changes.

We laugh about it now, but during that week, the realization hit us that there was not a work force out there that could perform the quality of work that Maryanne demanded. Without good cutters, we were out of business, or even worse, we were in a business that put us in the same league as the salons who were cutting all of the fans' hair at the Astrodome, and that was totally unacceptable to Maryanne, who is herself a master haircutter.

(In fact, over the years, we have spent more than $65,000 on Maryanne's haircutting education. She has studied all over the world with the best haircutters and teachers, including Vidal Sassoon and Paul Mitchell. She is an expert not only in haircutting itself but also in the "chemical" area, which includes hair coloring, permanents, etc. She also worked with our chemists in formulating our current line of hair-care products, called "In Salon–Liquid Tools".)

Nevertheless, on Day One, as I mentioned earlier, we were faced with a problem that we hadn't anticipated but had to solve immediately. If we couldn't hire the people we needed, we'd have to train them ourselves. We started out by setting up our first "school" at the Greenspoint salon itself, with Maryanne shuttling back and forth between New York and Houston, running her salon in New York and teaching classes to new recruits in Houston.

Although our haircutters were getting better, both Maryanne and I agreed that until they reached the level of professionalism that we believed our customers deserved, we could not in good conscience charge for our haircuts. We decided to give them away for free. Come one, come all.

I would venture out into the mall, look for someone who

The Tools: Don't Leave Home without Them

appeared to need a cut, introduce myself, make my free offer—which they found hard to believe—and rope them in. To this day, during slow periods our haircutters still go out and "recruit" customers into their chairs. We're very aggressive, but when you're giving great haircuts—and you know it—you've got the confidence to do things that you never thought you could do. I think one of the great shortcomings in American retailing or the restaurant business is that the management stops one step short of bringing its clientele into the stores. Especially for new business, you have to go out, literally find your customers, and drag them into your shop. It's not that difficult to do. It just takes a lot of hustle combined with a little humor.

Now I don't profess to understand the way information is passed throughout a network of individuals, but I once saw a segment on "National Geographic" that had to do with some species of monkey that inhabits the African savanna. Once one monkey gets the word that danger is afoot, within seconds the message is somehow transmitted to every other monkey in the pack, and moments later there is a monkey stampede in full progress. That's pretty much the way it happened at Greenspoint Mall.

Once the word got out about our free haircuts, people lined up by the hundreds, and we appeared to be the hottest shop in the mall. The good news is that our haircutters were getting the training—even if it was on the job—that they so desperately needed. The bad news was that while we appeared to be prosperous beyond our wildest dreams, in fact we weren't making a nickel.

Nevertheless, we had committed ourselves to the long-term view and long-term success, so if that meant putting off our profits for a few more weeks, so be it. We knew the profits would eventually come. Training had to come first.

Basic Training

Although it was the farthest thought from our minds at the time, giving away free haircuts turned out to be one of the most brilliant, ahem, marketing moves we ever made. Those hundreds of customers who received those free haircuts in our early months became our most loyal customer base, and today, thirteen years later, many of them are still coming to the same hairdresser who cut their hair originally for free.

What Maryanne put into place at Greenspoint, then, was the beginning of our formal training program at Visible Changes, which now has become the standard in our industry and blossomed into Visible Changes University. I think it's fair to say that at VCU we have the finest training program for haircutters in the industry. It's all because of Maryanne, who appears to be one of those "ordinary people" who achieves extraordinary success, over and over again.

Maryanne, like many women in her generation, is not comfortable with being on center stage. She has always been content to let me stand in the spotlight while she went quietly on her way, doing her job without hoopla or fanfare every day of every week of every month of every year. With Maryanne (and hopefully at Visible Changes), excellence has become ordinary.

While I eat, breathe, and sleep business twenty-four hours a day, Maryanne's commitment has always been to her craft: haircutting. In that regard, we make a good team, because she has the total respect of our haircutters—they know that she can do better what they do well—and I can concentrate on pushing my numbers around, people development, business opportunities, and reward and motivational programs for our staff.

In many regards, Maryanne is more of a pioneer than I am, since I've always had my Ray Krocs, Walt Disneys, and Vince Lombardis to look up to and to learn from. Maryanne had to achieve her success without much guidance from female role

The Tools: Don't Leave Home without Them

models. Increasingly, she has become a consummate role model herself—even on the small things.

When Maryanne changes her hairstyle, for example, hairstyles change throughout our company. When Maryanne trades in her old car for a new one, our parking lot changes accordingly. And, it's true, when Maryanne became pregnant the first time, a mini–baby boom took place throughout our company.

I think one reason that Maryanne and I have lived so well together and worked so well together for so many years is that we both were born and raised in lower-middle-class families with limited expectations for their children. In our cases, Maryanne and I each rebelled and decided we'd take our own chances by going our own ways.

Security, which was paramount to our parents, was nothing to us, since we were able to see that our parents had virtually no security at all. My dad worked at the same bank for more than thirty-eight years, never made more than ten thousand dollars a year, and could have been fired at the whim of any one of his superiors. That's security?

Maryanne was the youngest of seven children, all girls. Her mother was certain she would be a boy, and her name was to be Danny. Her mother was an orphan who cleaned people's houses and took in ironing to help make ends meet, especially when her father, who was a house decorator and painter, was out of work, which was often.

When I think about Maryanne's childhood and adolescence, I'm reminded of the thought that wildflowers can flourish in any environment.

Where this particular Wild Flower grew up was in my hometown of Queens Village, New York. Let me tell you a little bit more about Maryanne, whose own emphasis on training has translated into our fanaticism on the subject.

Basic Training

Maryanne went to St. Agnes Catholic High School, an all-girl school, where grades were second only to religion on the list of what would get you into Heaven. It took three separate bus changes and an hour of traveling time just to get from her home to St. Agnes. Every Sunday was church and confession. Her father was a fearsome figure who demanded good grades and total obedience, and rarely, if ever, showed any affection toward her or the rest of the family. Maryanne was terrified of him.

During her junior year in high school she was told by the guidance counselor that she would be very good with her hands. To her mother, that meant secretarial work, since Maryanne had two sisters who were secretaries with the FBI. To Maryanne's mother, this was a dream job: the total security of working for the government and an environment where her daughter would be surrounded by scores of handsome G-men. Further, Maryanne was always good in English and likes to tell people, with a fair quotient of honesty "I can spell, and John can add."

Like her mother, Maryanne was a tireless worker. At age sixteen, she got her first job selling chocolates on holidays at Wolfe's Candy Store and then worked at Food Fair as a checker after school, at night, and on Saturdays. She became the fastest (and was already the cutest) checker in the grocery store.

Maryanne's plan for herself was to go on to beauty school after high school to become a hairdresser. To her mother, that was pure insanity. Hairdressers, in her view, were one step below waitresses and one step above streetwalkers. The FBI was where a respectable young lady belonged.

Now Maryanne is as diplomatic as she is strong-willed, so in deference to her mother, she agreed to have at least an interview for a secretarial spot with the FBI.

She got up early, around 5 A.M., nervous about going into the big city, New York, from our tiny Long Island suburb of Queens

The Tools: Don't Leave Home without Them

Village. She put on her makeup carefully and chose her best dress. She wanted to make a good impression—even though she didn't really want the job. Her interview was scheduled for 9:00, so she got on the 7:30 bus, which dropped her off in midtown Manhattan, where she transferred to the subway.

That's when her troubles started. It was pouring rain, and she got on the wrong train. When she got out, her umbrella blew inside out, her makeup smeared, and as she ran, she broke her heel off her high-heeled shoes. She started crying, which made the makeup smear more, and by the time she got directions for the right subway, her stockings had big splotches of mud all over them. She arrived fifteen minutes late for the interview, looking like a total mess and crying her eyes out.

P. S.: Yes, she was offered the job (who says the FBI has no heart?) but turned it down to the utter dismay of her mother. She then went to work full-time at Food Fair to save the $200 down payment to start classes at the Queens Beauty School in Jamaica, Long Island. On her first day of beauty school, her mother unplugged her alarm clock so that she would oversleep. It was a clumsy attempt. Maryanne was up long before the clock had been set to go off. After her classes started, she cut back to part-time work so she could afford the $23-per-week tuition payment. Her Food Fair paycheck was $21, and her dad secretly gave her the extra $2 plus bus fare.

Her schedule was beauty school from eight to five each day, followed by a mad dash to catch the 5:05 bus to Food Fair in order to be at the register by 5:30. If she missed the bus, she was late for work, but of course she charmed the bus driver into waiting for her a few extra minutes when she was running late.

From the first day, she loved beauty school—hair, nails, pedicures, the whole nine yards—and she became, of course, very good at it.

Basic Training

In a totally unplanned and unconscious way, Maryanne took a shortcut to becoming one of the better hairdressers in the country. She adopted the "Do as I do method," attaching herself to role models who were extremely good at what they did and then simply imitating what they did. It's one of the fastest ways of shortening the learning curve. That's what teachers and masters and mentors are for.

I met Maryanne shortly after she accepted her first job in our industry, working as a shampoo girl in a small beauty shop in Bayside, Long Island. John McNulty, a mutual friend, gets the finder's fee. The romance itself began at Kelly's, a Queen's Village bar with a three-piece band, where all the locals hung out.

McNulty introduced us. She asked me what I did, and I told her I was a cop. I asked her what she did, and she said she was a hairdresser. I asked her how many heads she did in a day, and she said about a half dozen. I told her she was never going to get rich that way.

I followed up with an invitation to *The Sound of Music* and with the exception of one or two early stumbles on my part (involving my making a lot of money, limousines, and stewardess parties), Maryanne has always been there for me.

After I lost all my money, I was in bad shape, and I called Maryanne one night at about 2 A.M. from a phone booth near her apartment. She asked me where I was, and I told her I was thinking of lying down on the tracks at the subway station.

She ran down to the station and brought me back to her apartment. We talked all night, and I think it was that night that we made a total commitment to each other.

Our first venture turned out to be a salon called Raggedy Ann's. It was a real dump, but we couldn't afford to shut it down to remodel, so every Saturday night we would carry all of the furniture down to the basement so the workers could renovate,

The Tools: Don't Leave Home without Them

and the following week we would haul it back up. This went on for six weeks.

I was on the road selling washing machines for Bernie, and Maryanne was in charge of the business. Her emphasis from the outset was on training. During the day she would train her own operators and at night she'd go into New York City to take advanced training at the Sassoon School and the Paul Mitchell School. At that point in her life, Maryanne's dream was simply to be a better and better hairdresser—to keep up with all the new innovations and maybe someday get a larger and nicer salon.

Sales improved almost in lockstep with our quality, and as our quality improved, we raised our prices. Each night, Maryanne would put our excess profits into a shoe box in the kitchen, and one evening we counted the cash: $80,000. "Hmmm," I thought. "There might be a real business here after all."

Although I was making a high six-figure income selling washing machines, we continued to live in our $120-a-month walk-up flat on Borkel Place. (We now have the "Borkel Place" street sign mounted in our media room, and we go back to the old place from time to time.)

The $80,000 that had accumulated in the shoe box plus the weekly operating funds from Raggedy Ann's were the money we survived on for two years while we got Visible Changes going in Houston.

(I think it was Willie Sutton who, when asked why he robbed banks, responded, "Because that's where the money is." From our perspective, when people ask us why we decided to operate in shopping malls, as opposed to freestanding locations or strip centers, we respond that malls are where the people are, and Texas, in general, and Houston, in particular, probably have more shopping malls than anywhere else in the country. For us, it was the perfect place to set up shop.)

I can't tell you that we had long, philosophical conversations

Basic Training

about the importance of training to our operations. It was never really an issue. The fact is that Maryanne very simply would never stand for an ill-prepared haircutter getting his or her hands on a customer's hair. Her dedication to her craft simply made that an impossibility.

And, ultimately, I think that commitment to excellence has become responsible for our success. Over the years, of course, we've gotten better at it, since we've consistently raised rather than lowered our standards. Currently, approximately five cents of every dollar that Visible Changes earns goes into training, which is well over a million dollars a year—not including, of course, the cost of running our school.

While I take you through a typical training program for a Visible Changes recruit, I ask that you pay attention to the toughness of the program. Our methodology, simply put, is to team up these new staff members with masters in our field who can instruct them in the proper way to cut and perm hair and perform other duties. Then they do it over and over and over again, ad nauseum, until it becomes, literally, automatic.

Remember, even Liberace got started by running his digits clumsily across the black and whites, producing some of the most god-awful, discordant sounds known to humanity. Everything is difficult when it is new. Training and practice are what make the difficult easy and transform a foreign object, be it a computer, a pair of scissors, or a musical instrument, into an instrument of grace.

At the risk of slowing down this narrative for a minute or two, let me share with you a poem that illustrates my point. My coauthor, David Legge, keeps digging up these relics for me.

The Touch of the Master's Hand
'Twas battered and scarred, and the auctioneer
    Thought it scarcely worth his while

The Tools: Don't Leave Home without Them

To waste much time on the old violin,
　　But he held it up with a smile;
"What am I bidden, good folk?" he cried,
　　"Who'll start the bidding for me?
A dollar—one dollar—then two, only two—
　　Two dollars, and who'll make it three?
Going for three"—but no—
　　From the room far back, a gray-haired man
Came forward and picked up the bow;
　　Then wiping the dust from the old violin,
And tightening the loosened strings,
　　He played a melody pure and sweet
　　As a caroling angel sings.

The music ceased and the auctioneer,
　　With a voice that was quiet and low,
Said, "Now what am I bid for the old violin?"
　　And he held it up with the bow;
"A thousand dollars—and who'll make it two?
　　Two thousand and who'll make it three?
Three thousand once—three thousand twice—
　　And going—and gone," cried he.
The people cheered, but some of them cried,
　　"We do not quite understand;
What changed its worth?" Quick came the reply,
　　"The touch of a master's hand."

And many a man with life out of tune,
　　And battered and scarred with sin,
Is auctioned cheap to a thoughtless crowd,
　　Much like the old violin,
A mess of pottage—a glass of wine,
　　A game—and he travels on;
He's going once—and going twice—

Basic Training

> He's going—and almost gone!
> But the Master comes, and the foolish crowd
> Never can quite understand,
> The worth of a soul, and the change that's wro't
> By the touch of the Master's hand.
> —Myra Brooks Welch

In any event, on Day One of employment at Visible Changes, we spend three hours giving an overview of our company, its history, its current status, its values, and why we think it's so special. From the outset, we tell our new people the truth—what we expect of them, what we think they're capable of, and the rewards that will come to them if they make the effort and commitment.

We tell horrific stories of the "back room," where it's all tedium—sweeping, cleaning, and shampooing for hour after hour—adding that how long they remain there is totally up to them. Some have graduated onto the cutting floor in three months; others are still there six to nine months after coming to the company. We tell them that if they miss a class because their car broke down, that's another week in the back room. During this "boot camp" phase, there are no excuses.

I learned from Nick that if you give a good person a lousy job to do, he or she will work doubly hard to reach the good job that you have waiting in the wings for them. On average, it takes about three to six months to get out of our back room.

During that time, the staff members will have cut maybe 250 heads of hair (on nonpaying customers who act as models), as opposed to in an average salon, where he or she will have cut, literally, not one head of hair before starting on a customer—possibly you or your spouse.

(At Visible Changes University, our goal is to get our people up to one thousand haircuts before they become floor cutters.

The Tools: Don't Leave Home without Them

With that kind of expertise, we'll be able to meet our goal of raising our haircut prices by five to ten dollars in the next year or two.)

For these first three to six months, we simply drill, drill, drill, learning from the best in the business. We regularly bring in the best haircutters from around the world to perform and demonstrate their techniques for our people.

Our haircutters, and their haircuts, are frequently featured in the top industry and trade publications in the country; need I tell you the pride that this builds within our company?

But do you know what else happens as a by-product of all this training? From time to time, one of our top haircutters will leave for a better offer at another "hot" salon in our city, and, invariably, he or she will return. The self-discipline they learned at Visible Changes just can't be found among the competition, and our people miss it. It's like we're spoiling them for the rest of the work world. They know how good they can be, and they're unhappy with themselves when they're being anything less.

To be as good as we are, we always have to keep the intensity level up. At the most, there's probably less than 1 percent between being good and being great. To be great, you are the cutting edge. You're the razor.

At Visible Changes, of course, training is an all-the-time, forever undertaking. Everybody comes back to the corporate office for at least two days every two months for exhaustive and inspiring presentations by our top people. Mayolo, one of our managers who used to work in fashion retailing, will talk to them about dressing for success. Tony Hatty and Steven Waldon tell stories about changing their "born to lose" syndrome. Sandi Morton and Carl Fairman, our two regional managers, expose them to the novel idea that working hard can be fun and not working hard can be boring.

Basic Training

We show our newcomers videotapes of our company confer-
ences, and I tell them that if they want to commit to doing something important with their lives, then Visible Changes will commit
to being their partners. I tell them, in effect, that being successful
takes sacrifice, but there is a better life and a better value system
than most of them have been living. The system works, and it's
needed. Discipline never fails. What we've been talking about in
this book—discipline, conation, motivation, education, and training—are unbeatable qualities.

One of the greatest injustices I think can be done to young
people—especially those who opt to go to beauty school, since they
usually come from the lower end of the education and economic
spectrum—is to lure them into vocational school programs, full
of hopes and dreams and anticipation for the future, take the little
money that they have at their (or their family's) disposal, and then
graduate them into the work force totally untrained to practice
their profession. Being a former cop, I'd simply put scores of these
vocational school scoundrels in prison. You don't want to know
what Maryanne would do to them.

Let me close this by telling you one last story about Maryanne
and her mentor, Paul Mitchell, that is especially important to her
and, I think, instructive to all of us. Paul Mitchell probably has
done more to upgrade our business and professionalize it than
anyone else. He's known mainly for his products, of which he sells
more than $100 million a year, but to us in the industry, especially
haircutters such as Maryanne, he's been the "hairdresser's hairdresser." As I mentioned earlier, Maryanne studied under him
briefly in New York.

Anyway, Paul arrived one day at Visible Changes, unannounced, and asked Maryanne if she would show him our operations and our salons. She said she would but on one condition:
she wanted his honest opinion of our business—nothing but the

The Tools: Don't Leave Home without Them

unvarnished truth. She asked him to reserve his thoughts until he had seen all of our operations, and he agreed.

Maryanne was on cloud nine. Here she was with her hero, showing him *our* company and introducing him to *our* people. At the end of the day, over dinner, Maryanne told him, "Please don't hold back, Paul. I'm a big girl now, and I can take the criticism. I know that it's going to help me get better. I really want to improve upon what we're doing."

Then Paul looked at Maryanne and said, "Maryanne, let me tell you something. Years ago when I had Super Hair at Crimper's Salon in New York, this had been my dream. I wanted to take a chain of salons, have everybody cutting the same technique, and maintain quality control that way. But everybody told me that I couldn't do it, and I believed them.

"You did what was in my mind, and you not only did it, you did it successfully. Honestly, I can't tell you one thing that I saw wrong. The haircutting is fabulous. I see a little of my technique, and a lot of my training. It's exactly what I wanted to do. You've fulfilled my dream."

Paul Mitchell died a few months ago of pancreatic cancer, leaving to his partners a business empire worth a couple hundred million dollars and leaving to his industry a legacy of excellence.

On Paul's death, we created a plaque in his honor that hangs on our wall outside Maryanne's office. It was written by our regional manager Carl Fairman, one of the most creative people in our company. It reads:

> Friends remembered, remain forever friends.
> Artists having taught, go on to teach again
> through proud memories whispering loud lessons.
> Listen, swiftly listen.
> And remember.

Basic Training

> For swiftly pass the greatest lessons,
> Swifter still, the greatest men.
> And sifting through the mind's collections,
> Gather a dream.
> Capture a smile.
>
> Now the led become the leaders.
> From the students, teachers rise.
> Let the man not go forgotten
> when his message lives and thrives.
>
> His spirit never dies.

Action Plan

- **Concentrate on people's positive points, not on their negatives.**

When we first started Visible Changes, I had difficulty in dealing with some of our haircutters—especially the ones who were "far out." I couldn't identify with them (nor they with me). It was Maryanne who taught me always to look below the surface, and I soon learned that some of our strangest-looking people were the most honest, spontaneous, creative, and, yes, hardworking if they were given the tools and the opportunities to excel.

- **If you have an ambition that you really want to pursue, as Maryanne did, then pursue it.**

Please, please do not get to mid-life, or old age, and say, as so many of us do, "I wish I had done that." Give it your best shot now, and if it doesn't work, do something else.

The Tools: Don't Leave Home without Them

- **Every human being has an inborn right to be taught basic skills in one career area.**

If we don't teach people how to fish, they certainly will learn on their own how to steal your fish.

- **After any failure, the path back to success comes with a return to the basics.**

- **Upgrading the minimum standards for any company will upgrade the standards eventually for the entire industry.**

That's the idea behind Visible Changes University, and we believe that every sizeable company should, in one way or another, be in the education business.

- **All entrepreneurs need someone who believes in them enough to get them back on track during those inevitable times of frustration and doubt.**

For me, of course, it was Maryanne, and I think (and hope) I did the same for her. The fact is that business—and life—are just too difficult to navigate without a loved one by your side. Believe me, creating a business is a two-person process, and it is nurturing to, not destructive of, a relationship.

- **Consider carefully whether you need to "leave home" and change your environment to make your idea work.**

In my case, if I had attempted to do Visible Changes out of Queens Village, New York, my cronies would have always thought of me as a former cop who believed more in screwing around than in building a serious business. I like the axiom, "Sometimes you need to find a new playground and new playmates." The same

Basic Training

holds true for my immigrant friends. I'm convinced that many of them would never have become successful in their native country. The change of venue enabled them to change their own attitudes about themselves. They were not hindered by low expectations from family and friends.

- **If you work together with your spouse, try to stay out of each other's way.**

At Visible Changes, Maryanne's responsibilities and mine are well defined and separate. I am in charge of marketing, advertising, public relations, and money management. Maryanne is in charge of training, service, and quality control. To this day, we maintain offices at opposite ends of our corporate headquarters and work with our own staffs of secretaries and support people. In the truest and best sense, we complement each other, and we're always there for each other.

Chapter 9

Self-Discipline

ALL OF THE things we've talked together about throughout this book—mentorism, conation, motivation, education, training—are nothing more than verbal flights of fancy if they're not linked up to discipline, or, more accurately, self-discipline.

Self-discipline is what gets us to the church on time and what gets the project done right, on time, the first time. It is what turns the wish into the reality.

Self-discipline, more than any other quality, is the tool with which we fashion our successes in life. If we never learn to use this tool, our lives eventually will become unmanageable, if not disastrous.

Author Scott Peck will forgive me, I think, if I pass on a few of his choicest words from his best-selling book, *The Road Less Traveled:* "Discipline is the basic set of tools we require to solve life's problems. Without discipline we can solve nothing. With only some discipline, we can solve only some problems. With total discipline, we can solve all problems."

Emerson's dictum, as we noted earlier, was "Nothing great was ever achieved without enthusiasm." McCormack's dictum is "Nothing great was ever achieved without self-discipline."

What exactly is this abstract quality called self-discipline, and why is it in such short supply in modern-day America?

I define self-discipline as "the willingness to perform the acts that are beneficial to us that—for whatever reason—we don't want to perform."

Conversely, let me tell you what self-discipline is not: It is not genetic—something some of us were born with and others were not. It is not instinctual—something that comes naturally to us without effort.

The Tools: Don't Leave Home without Them

The good news about self-discipline is that it can be taught, modeled, and learned, and the bad news is that there are few teachers or role models in society to pass this most valuable commodity on to the next generation. Permissiveness is deadly poison to self-discipline, and a permissive society, such as the one in which we live, has relegated self-discipline to the endangered species list.

When wordsmith Woody Allen once philosophized that "80 percent of life is just showing up," he was talking about self-discipline.

Nevertheless, I am always amazed that when the attendance roll is taken among new staff at Visible Changes, how many of the new recruits are absent or late and appear totally unconcerned or unfazed by their lack of responsibility.

One of our managers, Cleta Gordon, who has been with Maryanne and me from the beginning, has interviewed hundreds, maybe thousands, of applicants over the last dozen years or so and offers this report:

"Most of these young men and women have breezed through the first twenty or so years of their lives without having acquired any sense of accountability or responsibility or, for the most part, even the most rudimentary academic or life skills.

"Most are still living at home where all their whims, wants, and perceived needs are still being provided for. They have never held a steady job, have never had to pay for their own food, clothing, rent, or transportation. In many cases, their mommies are still making their beds. They have been totally indulged and, consequently, are unprepared to enter the work force."

In a very real sense, these kids come to us both enabled and crippled. Their parents—out of neglect, ignorance, or a perceived need to protect their children—have unintentionally prepared them for a fantasy world that simply does not exist. In many cases,

Self-Discipline

the parents, too, have lived their own lives without any consistent sense of self-discipline and are ill-prepared to teach it to or model it for their children.

Remember, we are talking about a generation that has subscribed to the notion "Just say yes" to drugs, food, and alcohol. Three percent of all Americans, a recent study reported, are addicted to cocaine, and there are more than twenty million regular users. Estimates of full-fledged alcoholics range from thirty million to sixty million Americans—that's one out of every four men, women, and children. That's our work force that we're looking to to compete in the new global economy. As a nation, we're literally billions of pounds overweight. Take a trip to any shopping mall and observe the physical condition of the people who parade by.

Ask a child whether he or she would prefer a piece of chocolate cake that is fattening but pleasurable or a nice portion of spinach that is beneficial but distasteful, and the child will choose the cake every time. All too often, so will the parents.

As a country, America has been on a binge—physically, morally, intellectually, and economically—for so long that it is going to be very difficult to kick the indulgence habit. The idea that "recess is finally over" is becoming more, not less, unthinkable for most of the American public.

If what I've recited above is the bad news about the state of our country, the good news is that these ills can be cured, and the antidote, of course, is a healthy dose of self-discipline. The further good news is that the application of self-discipline can be made in a moment. It's not something we need to go to school for years to study. It can be summed up fairly well in the current popular ad campaign for Nike athletic shoes, built around the title, "Just Do It."

While I've been citing mainly negative evidence of a country on a bender, I always think that, after the diagnosis, it's more

The Tools: Don't Leave Home without Them

productive to look to the best, most productive, and most successful members of our society in order to formulate a cure.

Fortunately, there are signs that American industry, as well as the people who make it up, are getting fed up with the indulgence and permissiveness of the past. A recent front-page article in the *New York Times* related the story of a young woman who only a year ago wore a T-shirt with the message "Sex, Drugs, Rock & Roll." Today, she won't take it out of the closet, preferring instead one that advertises "Drug-Free Body."

The story goes on to tell of Hallmark cards with the message "I think you're a much neater person when you're not drinking," and a bakery in San Francisco that sends out fortune cookies with the message "Your discipline will be rewarded." Last, the article cites a cartoon in *The New Yorker* magazine of a middle-aged man declining an invitation: "We'd love to but we had too much wine and cheese in the '80s," he says.

Such books as *In Search of Excellence* by Thomas J. Peters and Robert H. Waterman, Jr., have become best-sellers by chronicling the inspirational stories of companies that became successful by going the extra mile. Recently "60 Minutes" did a feature story on Nordstrom department stores and the phenomenal lengths their staff go to to provide customer service—frequently on their own off-time. While the union is suing Nordstom to compensate these workers for their off-duty hours, staff member after staff member told "60 Minutes" that they were going the extra mile for the customer and for their employer simply because they wanted to. A move is now afoot at Nordstrom to decertify the union.

At Visible Changes, our whole program of training—some might even say indoctrination—is built around the concept of self-discipline. As I mentioned earlier, we take our new recruits (and it's no coincidence that I'm using military terminology here) and

Self-Discipline

begin their training in the "back room," shampooing hair, sweeping floors, and cleaning toilets. It's very much like the business equivalent to basic training in the military. The legend and lore of our company is replete with stories of how much tougher it was back when "our class" went through it in the olden days. Our experienced people tell us we're getting too soft.

Like basic training, our back room is a common experience that builds a bond among all of our staff—all of whom hate it at the beginning and later would not trade it for the world.

Our main purpose in starting people out in the back room, regardless if they were superstars in their former salons, is that we want our people to get into the habit of doing the same simple things (such as washing hair) over and over and over again, ad nauseum, until it becomes automatic. We want our people to do repeatedly something that they don't want to do. Most of them have never had to do that in their entire lives.

At this stage in their development, we want them to do unquestioningly whatever we tell them, and we're not particularly interested in their ideas of a better, or easier, way to do it. We know what works, and we know that what they've been doing with their lives and/or careers has not worked. Our way is the harder way, but it's the better way. It teaches self-discipline. It also gives the new staff an incentive to want to move onward and outward, onto the cutting room floor, faster, simply to get their back-room experience behind them. The better they do in the back room, the quicker they're out of there.

When Maryanne and I built Visible Changes, we ate, slept, and drank our business twenty-four hours a day. It was a total commitment, and it completely dominated our lives and our lifestyle. We didn't go out to movies, to the theater, to the country club, or to friends' homes for dinner. Frankly, living such an unbalanced life was a difficult and maybe even terrible sacrifice

The Tools: Don't Leave Home without Them

for us to make, but we didn't know any other way to do it, and, I'm sorry to report, we still don't.

Today, of course, we're reaping the benefits of those early years, and we do have the luxury of being able to travel and concentrate our work efforts on things that are fulfilling to us, but that is the nature of sacrifice. It's going without now for a benefit later. We never could have gotten Visible Changes off the ground without the self-discipline that we brought to the original start-up.

As another example, look at doctors. They sacrifice in school for maybe twenty-five years, studying relentlessly and postponing their career and oftentimes marriage and family life in pursuit of their profession. Do I begrudge them their large egos and outrageous fees? Not one bit.

Perhaps because of our own experiences at Visible Changes, Maryanne and I are relentless about instilling self-discipline in our staff. It probably is one of the most important things we do, other than offering them an opportunity to make a good living, because they will take those personal habits with them wherever they go. VC "graduates" are winners not just at work but in life.

How do we teach or instill self-discipline in our people? The same way Vince Lombardi did or a marine drill instructor does. We practice the fundamentals over and over and over until they become absolutely automatic—and then we practice them some more. We get so good at what we do that no one else is even in our league.

In sports at the Olympic level, the difference between first place and fifth place in the hundred-yard dash is, perhaps, one-tenth of a second. When one is cutting the onionskin this fine, what is the difference between winning and losing? Self-discipline, pure and simple. It's running that extra dash one more time after everyone else has gone home for the night. Can you

Self-Discipline

imagine how many laps Mark Spitz had to swim in order to bring home seven gold medals in the 1972 Olympics? Larry Bird, the superstar of the Boston Celtics, says the actual basketball season is a snap compared to his training program in the off-season. The thing that separates the winners from the losers, the stars from the superstars, is self-discipline.

It was billionaire H. Ross Perot (who, by the way, was my successor on the cover of *Inc.* magazine as "The Hottest Entrepreneur in America") who said that most of us quit at the one-yard line. We've already done 99 percent of the work necessary for success, and then, for whatever reason, we poop out and sabotage our victory.

I'm not enough of a psychologist to know why that is, but I do know enough Italian math to know the real profits are made in that last 1 percent of performance.

Think of a baseball player who, let's say, is batting .250 and his counterpart who is batting .333. The difference between these two players is only one hit in every twelve times at bat. One crummy hit every three games. And yet the .250 ball player might be taking home $300,000 per year, and the .333 player a million and a half—five times as much. That's a very expensive and worthwhile extra hit he's getting. Self-discipline is how he gets it. He simply works harder.

It's the same in business. I have a friend in Houston with higher name recognition than our mayor or the governor of the state of Texas. His name is Jim McIngvale, but he's known as "Mattress Mac." He owns a furniture store here called Gallery Furniture. Two years ago I had him speak to our staff at our company conference because his story was so incredible and inspirational.

Ten years ago, it seems, Mac and his wife moved to Houston from Dallas, where he had been a staff member in a furniture

The Tools: Don't Leave Home without Them

outlet. Going nowhere, he decided to forge out on his own and put to work what he had learned. He thought he could do it better.

He set up in Houston during the boom time, and just when he got his business going, the price of a barrel of oil plummeted, taking with it the Houston economy. Almost overnight, people were moving out of Houston, not into it, and selling their own furniture, not buying more of it from Mattress Mac. As his sales fell, his desperation increased. If he didn't do something fast, he was soon going to be in bankruptcy.

The something that Mattress Mac did was decide to take his last ten thousand dollars in cash and put it into television advertising. He couldn't afford to hire any actors, so, although he was painfully shy, he decided to buck up and do the commercial himself. He also had to write his own material since he couldn't afford to hire an advertising agency. The only time he could afford to rent a studio at one of the small independent stations in Houston was after midnight when the rates were low.

And so, Mattress Mac, with his knees quivering and body quaking, arrived at one in the morning at Channel 26 with his ten thousand dollars in hand. He was about to take his last shot.

He did the first thirty-second take—and it was terrible. So were the tenth take and the twentieth. It just wasn't working. He was nervous, desperate, exhausted, and stumbling over his lines. Finally, he ran out of time. The technicians were preparing to go home, he had spent a good portion of his money on the production, and he still had no commercial. He pleaded with the technicians to try it just one more time.

At the end of the final try—the one-yard line, if you will— Mattress Mac scored a touchdown. He got an inspiration. He reached into his back pocket, pulled out a bunch of his overdue bills, put them in his fist, jumped up in the air, and shouted, "Gallery Furniture really will SAVE YOU MONEY!"

It was, as they say, a take.

Self-Discipline

At first, the television station refused to air the commercial because it was so amateurish and "not up to our standards." But Mattress Mac insisted and persisted, and eventually it went on the air.

The rest is history. Today, some ten years later, Mattress Mac's local advertising budget is sixty thousand dollars *per week*. A Gallery Furniture commercial airs on either television or the radio every seven minutes, twenty-four hours per day, 365 days per year. Mattress Mac still writes and stars in all of the commercials himself and still ends each one by jumping up and shouting, "Gallery Furniture really will SAVE YOU MONEY!"

The kicker to the story is that I recently put together a three-day seminar at my house to which I invited the deans of some of the top business schools in the country, including Wharton, the University of Texas, UCLA, Notre Dame, and the University of Houston. Also invited were three separate panels of entrepreneurs (those with businesses doing $25 million or less in sales, $25 million to $50 million, and over $100 million). The purpose of the get-together was to try to educate the educators in the way successful entrepreneurs operate and to encourage them to include entrepreneurship as a major component of their undergraduate and MBA programs.

Mattress Mac joined us for one of the sessions and told the deans the story I just told you. He also admitted to them that he was currently experiencing a problem in his business; although he was now doing maybe $30 million in sales at his one location, he was sleeping only three hours per night. He wondered if they could help him with his management problem—which, in fact, they did.

What Mattress Mac didn't have, however, was a self-discipline problem. It was the one resource he could always count on to work for him, and it had made him a millionaire many times over.

When we broke up our session at 1 A.M. and everyone headed

The Tools: Don't Leave Home without Them

for his or her hotel room, I told Mac to get a good night's sleep because we were reconvening for breakfast at nine o'clock the following morning. Mac looked at me as if I were crazy. He said he wasn't going to bed but was headed for his warehouse, where he was going to move some furniture around with the workers to get it ready for his morning deliveries. Nevertheless, he said he'd join us at nine sharp for breakfast.

Contrast the Mattress Mac story with a lunch I had recently with one of my former business school students who was looking for some advice—and possibly some investment capital—regarding a venture he was considering starting. He had worked out his numbers, and they looked fine.

What didn't look fine to me, however, was the student. He had gained maybe fifteen pounds since I had last seen him, and, when the dessert tray rolled around, he was about to gain a few more. He acknowledged that he knew he probably shouldn't order up the éclair, but he went ahead and ordered and ate it anyway. The message to me was that here was a young man who was probably missing something in life. He knew what to do, but he didn't have the self-discipline to do it. It made me wonder and worry about what the rest of his life will be like and how he'll perform over the long haul in business.

Conversely, the employees of *The Washington Post*, who consistently put out one of the finest newspapers in the country, used to be, collectively, heavy smokers. It goes with the image of the profession, I guess. When the surgeon general released his report on the dangers of smoking, there were approximately five hundred reporters and editors puffing away in the fifth-floor newsroom. Today there are fewer than twenty. That takes self-discipline.

Now, in closing out this chapter, I want to take you through a little exercise involving self-discipline—your self discipline. It makes no difference what your record has been in the past,

Self-Discipline

whether you're just beginning your career or you're the head of a large company, or whether you're a housewife taking care of your kids and running a household. I want to prove to you that self-discipline is a state of mind, something you can access and apply whenever you choose, for your own benefit.

I want you to think of something difficult that you've been putting off, something that would be in your own best interest to begin and follow through on. It could be something physical, such as losing thirty pounds; athletic, such as competing in a 10K race; academic, such as enrolling in night school and earning an MBA; or something involving your career, such as applying for and obtaining a new position.

Identify and select a substantial goal, something that will make you feel good about yourself when you accomplish it and will bring about a major improvement in your life.

Next, get a yellow legal pad and take ten minutes to formulate exactly how you are going to reach your goal. Be sure you identify each of the tasks necessary to get you to your destination. Now add the all-important time element: Write down exactly when you are going to do this activity. If it's a training program to lose weight or run in a race, for example, how many days per week will you work out, and, as important, what hours during those days will you be at the gym or on the track? Be specific.

At this point, take a few moments to determine all of the benefits you will receive from accomplishing your goal. These might include better health, increased self-esteem, a better job, more status, or whatever else you can come up with. The idea is to link in your conscious mind, and later in your subconscious, the accomplishment of your goal with all of the benefits you will enjoy.

Now do the opposite: Write down all of the negative consequences you will experience if you do not make the necessary

The Tools: Don't Leave Home without Them

effort to accomplish your goal. These might include remaining in a dead-end job, having continued health problems, feeling shame about your appearance, etc. Again, make this list as comprehensive as you possibly can. The idea, of course, is to link painful associations to not accomplishing your goal.

Last, take approximately five minutes to sit in a quiet place by yourself and focus deeply and narrowly on what you have written. Internalize as best you can the positive and negative consequences of reaching, or not reaching, your goal. Commit privately to yourself that this one goal in your life is the one thing that is not negotiable. If you're going to be running at 7 P.M. each evening, nothing, absolutely nothing, will get in the way of your doing so. This time is for you, this goal is for you, and this accomplishment is for you.

Begin each day by reading over what you have written on your legal pad. You might want to make a smaller wallet-sized version to carry with you and read from time to time in private. Then, at the appointed hour, to quote our favorite Nike ad, "Just Do It."

The good news is that self-discipline gets easier, not harder, with practice, but it is important to start with just one major goal. Almost immediately—probably on the first day of the new you—you will begin to feel better about yourself. You'll be smiling more, and no one will know why. But you will. It's because you've finally taken control of your own life!

Action Plan

- **Self-discipline is the one personality trait that virtually guarantees success, and the lack of it virtually guarantees failure.**

With self-discipline, anything is possible. Without it, nothing worthwhile is possible.

Self-Discipline

- **Self-discipline does not come naturally.**

In fact, it is contrary to our natural instincts. We are born seeking pleasure rather than pain, but maturity and growth require that we embrace our pain by meeting and grappling with our problems head-on. That requires self-discipline.

- **We develop self-discipline by imposing purpose, structure, and regularity on our lives.**

We need to establish what needs to be done, assign enough time to get the job done properly, and then, at the established time, "Just Do It."

- **99 percent of all people fail on the 99th yard.**

They simply don't have the self-discipline to finish the task and score the touchdown.

- **The real rewards in life are made by performance at the margins.**

Remember, the difference between a ballplayer hitting .250 and .333 is only one more hit for every 12 times at bat.

Part Four

Upward Bound

Chapter 10

The Savings Grace

I WANT TO open this chapter with the observation that most American corporations have their compensation programs set up exactly backward, and most staff expend their income exactly the reverse of how they should be spending it.

The employers try to shortchange their staff in order to keep more for themselves or to make the bottom line look better for their shareholders. "Pay them as little as possible" is the guiding principle. At Visible Changes, we "Pay them as much as possible," and do you want to know something? It works!

Likewise, on the employee side, the national norm is "Spend as much as possible"—that is, as much as you make plus as much as your credit will allow you to spend. At Visible Changes, our credo is "Save as much as possible, and live on as little as possible," and do you want to know something? It works!

At first, when writing this book, I thought long and hard about whether to downplay or even include the concept of the "20 Percent Rule." You will recall that one of the lessons I learned from my foreign friends was that in order to be successful, you have to have the discipline and the willingness to sacrifice to the extent of living on 20 percent of your income—and saving the remaining 80 percent.

I must confess to you that I've never had a good experience before a large audience—or any audience—when I've introduced the 20 Percent Rule.

Up until that point in my talks, I can be rolling along with my stories of Abe on the beach, Bernie's washing machines, and Nick's meatballs, but when I get to the question of saving—especially savings of the 80 percent variety—the audience looks at me as if I were talking a foreign language or have taken leave of my senses. At best, they think I'm talking symbolically or metaphorically, but certainly not seriously.

"It simply can't be done," "Not with my wife, you don't!", and "Have you pushed the numbers on this?" are the predictable responses.

And yet, I'm totally serious about the concept, and I know it can be done because I've done it for more than twenty years—both when I was making next to nothing and now that my income is substantial. In fact, when we were living in our $120-a-month walk-up on Borkel Place, our neighbors were incredulous when I told them my income from selling washing machines for Bernie was well into the six figures. They thought I was either crazy to live in such a dump when I could afford so much better—or that I was a liar.

You see, I believe that the extent to which we save and handle money can be looked upon as the indicator of how serious we are—or are not—about our lives. It says a lot about our optimism and how we as a people view our future.

In fact, a society that doesn't save is basically a society that doesn't believe it has any future—so why not get it all now? Live for the day, eat, drink, and be merry, so to speak, for tomorrow we shall die.

That would be fine if we all died tomorrow, but the fact is that most of us don't. We have to wake up with the results of our bacchanalian appetites: overweight, hung over, anything but merry, and deeply in debt.

Therefore, I think it is important to note that Americans save less of their paychecks than any people in the industrialized world—about 4 percent. The Japanese save four times as much. Visible Changes staff save at more than two-and-one-half times the Japanese rate—and still not nearly enough.

American banks are going broke because of our low savings

The Savings Grace

rate. Of the world's twenty largest banks, fourteen are Japanese, and only one, Citicorp, is American. In fact, only four out of the fifty largest banks in the world are American. To quote one analyst, America has become a "pygmy among giants" in the world of banking. We're simply no longer players.

By contrast, the largest bank in the world, the Japanese Dai-Ichi Kangyo, or "DKB," as it is known, is almost anachronistic by American standards since it is built predominantly on the weekly savings habits and deposits of millions of Japanese workers who make it their first stop after receiving their paychecks on payday. In America, the first stop too often is the local saloon. After all, it's Friday night!

While most of the industrialized world is building up its savings accounts, we're building up our credit card accounts. At the last tally, our total consumer debt—we're talking here the monthly Sears, Visa, and MasterCard bills—was close to $10 trillion.

We're awash in 850 million credit cards, with an outstanding balance of $1,600 for every man, woman, and child in the country.

"If you think money can't buy you happiness, you're shopping at the wrong malls," so the slogan goes.

Untold millions of Americans who appear outwardly prosperous and happy, are, in fact, technically bankrupt (they cannot afford to pay the interest payments on their debt) and, consequently, inwardly miserable.

It was the poet W. H. Auden who wrote, "Through headache and worry, life leaks slowly away." And, of course, what people worry most about is money. If it's true that an individual or a family—or a country—is as sick as its secrets, then America is indeed in trouble, because the true state of the financial affairs of most of us is our secret shame. It may shock you to hear how many successful businessmen I know who earn, say, in excess of $200,000 a year, yet couldn't put their hands on $5,000 in cash in a pinch. I'm telling you what you already know: it's no way to live.

It's been said that business school students really learn the lessons of cash flow and "playing the float" not by spending hours in lecture halls, but by juggling the balances due on their Visa and MasterCard.

"Let's see, I paid Visa last month, so this month I can charge more on the Visa, which will allow me to pay MasterCard, which in turn will allow me to charge more on the MasterCard, so next month I can pay Visa. . . ." And on and on. Once we step aboard this merry-go-round, regardless of our income, the whirlwind gets going faster and faster to the point that it's almost impossible to get off.

As our income increases, our definition of the term *necessities* likewise broadens accordingly. The fundamental rule is that our definition of "necessities" always grows slightly faster than our income. Let's look at a somewhat farcical, but all too typical, example of how most people handle success and the financial rewards that go with it.

Let's just say that up to this point, you've been paying attention, you've taken all my advice, and you've put into practice all of what I've been trying to teach you—and lo and behold, you find yourself making $200,000 a year, well on your way to your first million dollars.

If you're like most, you might take $100,000 and use it as a down payment on a $1 million home, since that's entirely do-able in today's mortgage market. Congratulations, my friend, you've just incurred a $900,000 debt with astronomical monthly payments!

But you're just getting started.

The house, of course, has to be furnished, and who would ever think of furnishing a $1 million house oneself. You'll need an

The Savings Grace

interior decorator for that, and your mate has heard that Mr. Pierre did such wonderful things for that neighbor of yours down the street ("who has no taste at all"), and that he's worth every penny of his outrageous fees.

The furnishings, of course, must be carefully selected (many of them imported), and somehow that old Buick that's been hauling you around just fine no longer seems to fit in your circular driveway. The Mercedes salesman, after one glance at your address, is only too happy to arrange financing on the latest 560SEL model.

Then there is the gardener to look after the lawn, the caterer to prepare the food to serve the guests ("What's the use of having this house if we can't show it off to our friends?"), the aproned "help" to serve the food, and, of course, the teams of maids to clean up after the repast.

All makes sense so far.

Then there is the obligatory wardrobe upgrade. Certainly Saks and Neiman Marcus will be more than happy to offer you his-and-hers credit cards (no limit), and, after all, how can you and your spouse expect to tool around in your new Mercedes 560SEL if you aren't dressed in the latest Armani and Bill Blass ensembles, accented by a simple, but traditional, Louis Vuitton purse (the original, of course; the people at the club can spot a vinyl imitation at a hundred yards)?

Oh yes, the club. The dues alone each month are more than you were paying for rent two years ago. But it's good for business lunches, golfing with clients, and, overall, "making connections." Right? Right.

Then, of course, there are the private schools for the kids (well, you wouldn't expect us to send young Winthrop into the blackboard jungle you've been describing throughout this book, would you, McCormack?).

And then there are the psychiatrist's fees ($125 for "fifty-minute hours"), which are explained to you in this way: "The more you pay, the better it is for your recovery."

Of course, it's decided soon after a few of these on-the-couch sessions that the children, too, need therapy. Sending them off to boarding school, it is suggested, might have had something to do with their hostile feelings toward you.

About this time, the concept of charity work will begin to preoccupy you and/or your spouse. You'll have to choose between the diseases or the arts, but, regardless of the choice, be prepared to pay big bucks. A table of ten at one of these black-tie fund-raisers can easily set you back ten thousand dollars, and that doesn't include the new suit or gown, the limousine, or the new haircut, not to mention the contribution that will get you into the fine print in the back of the program and into the social columns of the newspaper.

Oh, by the way, the dog, too, will have to go, since that faithful, but mangy, old mongrel simply no longer fits in with your new life-style.

This nightmare ends, of course, with the biggest expense of all, and that is for the divorce lawyers who are eager to go at it hammer and tongs to divide up (largely among themselves) what little remains of your once-great fortune.

In a word, we need to get back to the fundamentals of handling money.

First, think of accumulating and managing money as a *process*, not as an event. The hard reality is that you're not going to win the lottery, you're not going to strike oil, and you're not going to invent the next hula hoop. Remember how my friend Big Jim in Ann Arbor, Michigan, got rich? Simply by putting his nickels and dimes together, investing in something he believed in, and then sticking with it over the long haul.

The Savings Grace

What I'm going to explain to you is how to become and remain financially secure over the long term. Sure, I was a millionaire by age twenty-four, but, given what I knew then, there was not a chance that I could have sustained any level of long-term financial security. Not only had I drifted too far away from the fundamentals, I didn't even know what the fundamentals were. Now I do. Here they are:

What Nick taught me, and what all wise men and women know, is that *sacrifice* and *saving* are the two essential ingredients for long-term success, peace of mind, happiness, and contentment. Sacrifice, for our purposes, simply means delaying gratification today for a greater good tomorrow. Saving simply means taking a portion of every dollar you earn and stowing it away for security or future investment needs.

It's worth quoting a few paragraphs from a jewel of a little book by George S. Clason, *The Richest Man in Babylon,* in which he outlines in parable form the laws of financial success. It seems that the Babylonians were getting restless because the gold of that ancient land had fallen into the hands of a few while most of the population lived in poverty.

The king, seeing this as a threat, called to his throne Arkad, the richest man in Babylon, and asked him to share with his countrymen the secrets to his success. Arkad agreed to do so, suggesting that he gather one hundred teachers around him so that he could impart his knowledge unto them, and they in turn could educate others, who in turn would educate still more.

On the first day of their tutelage, Arkad turned to a poor egg merchant and asked him the following question:

> "If thou select one of thy baskets and put into it each morning ten eggs and take out from it each evening nine eggs, what will eventually happen?"

"It will become in time overflowing. . . ."

Arkad turned to the class with a smile. "Does any man here have a lean purse?"

First they looked amused. Then they laughed. Last they waved their purses in jest.

"All right," he continued, "now I shall tell thee the first remedy I learned to cure a lean purse. Do exactly as I have suggested to the egg merchant. For every ten coins thou placest within thy purse take out for use but nine. The purse will start to fatten at once and its increasing weight will feel good in thy hand and bring satisfaction to thy soul.

"Deride not what I say because of its simplicity. Truth is always simple. I told thee I would tell how I built my fortune. This was my beginning. I, too, carried a lean purse and cursed it because there was naught within to satisfy my desires. But when I began to take out from my purse but nine parts of ten I put in, it began to fatten. So will thine."

Arkad goes on to share with those assembled a fact that I have found true in real life, namely that when you put aside a portion of your income on a regular basis, two things mysteriously happen.

First, you don't miss the money you're saving. Somehow you manage to get along just as well, continue to pay your bills on time, and feel better about yourself because you are building up a "rainy-day" fund that gives you an increased sense of security.

Second, again as Arkad points out, people with money in reserve seem to attract more money from outside sources. It's the "rich get richer" syndrome, and it's true. While this appears mysterious to Arkad, I believe the phenomenon takes place simply because people with security, i.e., money in the bank, are more confident and have a healthier mind-set than those who are living on the edge, and that naturally attracts other people, such as

The Savings Grace

investors and deal-doers, to them. In any event, the benefits and rewards of regular savings far outweigh the sum total of the dollars that accumulate in the bank.

Now let us return to our $200,000-a-year executive (let's assume for the moment that he's male), and let's assume the worst: he's lost his job (as many hundreds, if not thousands, of Houston executives did when oil prices crashed in the early eighties).

Without warning, he is out of work. The cash flow stops, but the monthly payments do not. He has no financial reserves and is overextended to the hilt.

First comes denial (this can't be happening to me), then anger (after I gave them all of my best years), then shame (I can't let my friends know), and then reality:

He has to sell his home and cars, take his children out of private schools, quit his clubs, and, most likely, inform his wife that she will have to re-enter the work force.

(In many cases in Houston, the guilt and the shame accompanying this transition from the appearance of being rich to the reality of being poor were more than many men, women, and marriages could endure. There were many suicides and countless divorces.)

Now let us consider an alternative scenario:

Let's assume that for the last five years, our executive has been making the same salary, but has managed his income as follows:

First, and without fail, he's been putting 25 percent, or $50,000 per year, into savings (to keep our numbers simple, we'll omit interest income). Of course, he also pays Uncle Sam his due, which is another $50,000 per year. He's now got $100,000 per year, which is plenty, to live on.

Now let's examine what happens in this example when our executive is called in to receive the bad news:

First, he has a quarter-million dollars in the bank, or enough to continue his current life-style without interruption for two-and-one-half years, if he just goes to the beach every day. There is no need to sell the house or the cars, or put the kids into the middle of the blackboard jungle we've been describing. Simply put, there is no crisis.

In addition, if our executive is able to get another job at even half of what he had been making, he can continue his life-style literally forever, never even touching the $250,000, since he had already been living on 50 percent of his income.

(Of course, I would recommend a further reduction in expenditures of, say, up to 25 percent so that he could go on with his healthy habit of regular savings, but the main point is that he and his family continue to live within their means and without worry and fear.)

Now I ask you, which way do you want to live your life?

Saving-before-spending, which is a foreign concept to most Americans, is exactly the principle that immigrants embrace to make it in America. There is an irony in here somewhere.

If you take nothing else with you from reading this book, please take this principle: **Save before you spend.**

If you don't adopt this principle, you'll never be able to enjoy the house you live in, regardless of how lavish, the cars you drive, regardless of how luxurious, or even your own children, regardless of your best intentions, because you're always going to have to be on the line, eating Maalox and Excedrin, trying to make the next thousand dollars or desperately needing the next raise. Is anything worth that?

At Visible Changes we pay our staff so that fully 40 percent of all of their income is deferred (six months for bonuses and superbonuses, and to retirement time or the time they leave the company for profit sharing).

What most of us fail to realize is that our prime income-producing years are relatively few, say, from thirty-five to fifty-

The Savings Grace

five. Before that time we are learning or apprenticing, and after that time, we simply cannot count on having the energy, the drive, or the good health to be as productive as we once were. I'm not saying that there are not notable exceptions to this rule—I've already remarked that Ray Kroc didn't really "start" McDonald's (he actually acquired it from the McDonald brothers in California) until he was fifty-two—but clearly the Ray Krocs of this world are the exceptions.

To prepare yourself for the opportunities that are likely to come your way in business, you must have the cash resources on hand. Likewise, if living on a monthly Social Security check is as appetizing to you as it is to me, you simply must begin to save now for your less-productive years later.

The point here is to prepare, through hard work, savings, and investment, for a comfortable, but reasonable, life-style that you will be able to live forever. Therefore, if you don't own the company, someone might be able to take away your job, but they'll never be able to take away your family's life-style. To me, that's security.

If living on a portion of your income is Rule No. 1, Rule No. 2 is "Stay away from credit." While it's true that you need credit cards if you travel, they should be used for no other purpose. Get in the habit of paying cash for everything, with the possible exception of your house (for tax purposes only). Your monthly bills should be limited to your utilities, plus your mortgage or rent payment. Period. No car payment. No Saks payment. No Neiman's payment.

My father worked for the same bank for thirty-eight years, and, in fact, saved a small portion of his small salary. I still have memories of my mother doling out 40 cents to him each morning: 15 cents for bus fare each way to and from the bank and a dime for a soft drink to go with the lunch he carried each day in a sack.

Ask him why he stayed in the same job for nearly half a

century? He'll answer, I promise you, "Security." Some security. My father had become so risk-averse (as had many people who had gone through the Depression) that he stayed in a dead-end job forever.

I remember saving up one hundred dollars from an after-school job and giving it to my father on his birthday to buy himself a new business suit. The only restriction I put on the transaction was that he was going to have to give me back the change, because I knew that if he got to keep it, he would never be able to force himself to spend that much on himself.

In any event, coming from scrimp-and-save backgrounds, as both Maryanne and I did, we decided from the outset that Visible Changes would have to be planned as a company that could provide a decent living wage for our people.

We knew that if we offered six- or eight-dollar haircuts, as many of the chains, such as Fantastic Sam's, now do, there would be no way we would be able to pay our people a wage that would allow them to live with dignity and raise their families properly. Too many business owners too often forget that their employees have the same needs, wants, and desires that they themselves have. They want nice cars, a nice place to live, the opportunity to eat out at fine restaurants from time to time, the ability to buy birthday and Christmas presents for their children and family, and so forth.

Therefore, it was always our intention to start a business that would give our people the opportunity to have the very things that Maryanne and I wanted for ourselves and our children. Paying our people well became a fundamental premise of our business, and we aren't doing it totally out of philanthropy or altruism.

Quite the contrary. We realized that Visible Changes could never succeed if we couldn't pay our people a decent living wage. Eventually they would quit, move on, or leave the haircutting profession entirely. We would never be able to maintain a stable, loyal staff, which, in fact, is one key to our success.

The Savings Grace

And so, we began with the premise that we had to enable our people to do high-volume, high-quality work at reasonable prices, that is, the equivalent of a hundred-dollar haircut for thirty dollars.

That decision assured us healthy margins, if we could convince the customers to pay our prices, which led us to our next key decision:

In the past, the haircutting industry had been paying its cutters 50 percent commission on each haircut they produced. My own managers told me I was crazy when I told them I was going to pay our people lower commissions but they would make higher wages. In effect, I put into place a 25/35 percent formula in which a haircutter would make 25 percent commission on walk-in business and an additional bonus of 10 percent if the customer requested that particular cutter. Frankly, this "bonus" system encouraged our cutters to court their clients, and I believe to this day that it's been one of the keys to our success.

But, I was told in the beginning, no haircutter would work for a maximum commission of 35 percent.

I disagreed and, frankly, relied on my Wall Street experience for the formula. At the very time my own Wall Street firm was attempting to woo top account executives by increasing its commissions, its competitor, Merrill Lynch, was *lowering* its commissions but at the same time increasing training, advertising, and research support. The strategy worked. Business increased dramatically, the whole pie got bigger, and everyone got richer. That's the way it's worked for us, too.

Don't misunderstand me. We are tough bosses at Visible Changes, with high standards and high expectations for ourselves and our staff. The only thing we give away at our company is opportunity. Everything else is earned. Even our health benefits must be earned by selling $125 or more worth of retail products per week. (Not coincidentally, we do approximately four times the industry average in retail sales.)

While our people must earn everything they get, we have made it a company fetish to provide them with the best management and marketing tools available to perform their best work. Even our scissors are the best on the market—and they should be, at a hundred dollars a pair!

Likewise, on the business side we have put together a computer company, called "STATS Plus," staffed totally by Asian-American software specialists, most of whom have Ph.D.'s or MBAs. They have developed a touch-screen computer program that allows us to capture more information on our customers than any other institution I know of, other than the FBI.

Each year nearly 350,000 of our customers receive birthday cards, anniversary cards, and Christmas presents from us, which in turn builds customer loyalty, which results in higher paychecks for our people. Everybody wins.

As I mentioned earlier, for the first two years after Maryanne and I started Visible Changes, neither of us took out a dime in salaries or expenses. By the end of the third year, when we finally made our first profits of $106,000, we decided to give it back to our people in the form of profit sharing. Today, our profit sharing—which is nothing more than a "forced savings" account— has grown to nearly $8 million, and anyone who has been with us from the beginning has a nest egg waiting for him or her of well over $100,000.

Do you want to know something?

It works!

Action Plan

- **Adhere to the 20 Percent Rule. Live on less than you earn, and save or invest the rest.**

If you don't save, you'll never be free from worry, you'll never be happy, and you'll never be successful. Some things in life have a

The Savings Grace

"multiplier effect" (one action leads to many good results), and saving is one of them. The day you start saving, you'll feel better about yourself, you'll be more confident, and you'll be on the right track.

- **Stay away from credit, even (especially!) if it's offered to you.**

One of the sad truths is that people will give you things in life that are very bad for you. That's the way the Devil with his apple got his big break in the Garden of Eden. It's the same way with credit. It looks tasty, but it's poison.

- **Prepare for the hard times ahead.**

Countries get in trouble the same way people do—by spending more than they take in—and our federal government has been on such a spending binge for so long that our leaders have given up on financial dieting. A national economy that is in trouble, and ours is, eventually will experience higher inflation, higher taxation, unemployment, and a host of other bad things.

- **The successful countries of the future, like the successful people, will not be the ones with the highest standards of living today but the ones with the highest savings rates.**

- **A good definition of success is becoming self-sufficient through earning and saving so that "rainy days" or emergencies have no effect on your living standard or peace of mind.**

Nick believes that whatever happens in your business—even if it's cataclysmic—should not affect your family's living standard for at least three years.

- **At Visible Changes, we pay our staff well, and our staff have learned to save a disproportionate share of their income.**

That also benefits our company because our people are strong, financially viable, and, therefore, independent and secure enough to concentrate on their jobs without undue worry or stress. Our company—and our people—are better off for it.

- **Get involved with your finances.**

For some reason, people seem to be more embarrassed about money than they are about sex. Most people don't know a debit from a credit or an APR from an IRA. Money need not be a mystery. It's really very simple, but it does take a little bit of involvement, commitment, and study—after all, doesn't anything worthwhile?

Chapter 11

The Challenge

THE PURPOSE OF this book never was to make success look easy for you. It was to make success *possible* for you. If I could make success easy for you, I would be cheating you out of its biggest dividend, and that is the sense of awareness and aliveness and empowerment and, ultimately, self-confidence that can only come from confronting your problems head-on, rising, despite your fears, to their collective challenges, and ultimately prevailing. Vince Lombardi, of course, called this winning. There are few better feelings in the world.

In this book's introduction, I forewarned you: "The fundamentals you will learn in this book work *only if you work.*" Now, as we approach the close of this book, it is time to go to work.

All of my ruminations on all of these pages—in fact, all of the ruminations on all of the pages of all of the books that have ever been written on success or self-improvement, in business or in life—are nothing more than verbiage unless they can be upgraded into action. In this final chapter, you're going to take action. You're going to put into practice many of the things that we've talked about in this book, but you're going to do it without a lot of introspection or theorizing or philosophizing or even thinking. You're going to "Just Do It."

What you are about to do, I want to stress, is not an exercise. Too often we act as if today is simply a dress rehearsal for the play that is to come tomorrow, thereby putting a protective filter between ourselves and our lives. No, what I'm going to ask you to do today is the real thing, the main event.

If you're like most of the people I meet, your past and your present are seriously interfering with your getting on with your future. Believe me, I understand this. When I owed a quarter-million dollars at age twenty-six and saw no way I could ever crawl out of that financial hole, I had nothing to look forward to— not a hope in the world that I even had a future. I thought I was alone. What I didn't realize was that I was part of the majority! A recent opinion poll revealed that 60 percent of the American people report that they frequently *can't cope* because of anxiety, stress, and worry. Sixty percent! Think of that amount of mental devastation privately or secretly hidden within our society. Talk about a national secret shame.

On the other hand, Harry S Truman once said that in spite of his presidential duties and enormous responsibilities, he slept like a baby nearly every night of his tenure in the White House. Why? Because, he said, he faced his problems, one at a time, as soon as they presented themselves on his desk or in his personal life. Get the bad stuff over with so you can enjoy the good stuff, was Harry's way of thinking.

In my case, I just didn't see any way in which a high school graduate, meaning me, could ever get beyond a $250,000 debt.

Abe had the answer because Abe had a different perspective. First, to Abe, $250,000 wasn't all that much money. Anybody with half a brain could make $250,000, Abe said, and although at that time I thought he was half-crazy, the more I began to believe in him and the more I began to believe in myself, the more I realized that he was right.

As I write these words, the IRS has just reported that there are nearly a million and a half millionaires in the United States! Do you think all of these people are smarter than you are? If you believe that, they probably are—but I doubt it. As psychologist Abraham Maslow once said, "Why not you?" The important thing to remember is that you already have within you what it takes to become successful. What's been missing, for whatever reason, has been your willingness or ability to apply it.

The Challenge

When you don't use a muscle over a long period, it doesn't just rest. It atrophies. Likewise, once you begin to exercise your muscles, be they mental or physical, they get stronger, you gain confidence, and the next outing is easier, not harder, than the last.

Therefore, as they say at the Olympics, "Let the games begin."

My fear is that while I've been talking throughout this book about the basic ingredients of success—persistence, self-discipline, savings, motivation, education, training, and the like—there might be some very real impediments standing between you and where you want to be, just as there was for me with my quarter-million dollar debt.

I go back to that W. H. Auden quote: "Through headache and worry, life leaks slowly away." In this chapter, I want to help you plug the leak.

I want you to write down right now the three most difficult things in your life that you need to face but have been avoiding. These are things that are causing you pain, worry, sleeplessness, feelings of helplessness, shame, embarrassment, maybe even thoughts of suicide.

Maybe you need to fire a longtime employee who might also be a friend; maybe you need to break up a business partnership; maybe you've been afraid to answer your telephone because it might be someone calling to whom you owe some money; maybe you've been avoiding the IRS.

Whatever your "maybe" is, write down the three most troubling things that, if they were taken care of, would make your life immeasurably better immediately. Remember, the first (and toughest) step of any process is coming out of hiding.

Problems, when put off, grow in our minds until they are all out of proportion to their real seriousness. We lose our perspective.

I want to illustrate this.

A young lady who works on our staff was in such mental anguish that she came to me one day and told me her automobile had been repossessed because she had missed two consecutive payments. She was depressed and related that she also had gone haywire with her credit cards and now owed approximately $5,000 for past purchases.

Consider how powerful this process of "horrible-izing" and "catastro-phizing" can be. Here was a wonderful woman with family and friends and every possibility of a wonderful life, who was distraught with herself because she owed five-thousand bucks and a couple of car payments.

How many of us are in similar situations?

Of course, I could have given her the five-thousand dollars, but by now, you know that that is not how I operate.

I knew she had been with Visible Changes for seven years and upon further investigation I learned from our accounting department that she had accumulated $55,000 in her profit sharing account—which she hadn't even taken into consideration. In fact, her total debts were less than 10 percent of her net worth—far better than most Americans whose debts far outdistance their assets.

The first thing we did was put together a plan by which she would make payments from her Visible Changes salary to pay off all of the credit card bills within six months. Then we got one of our Visible Changes scissors and cut up her credit cards, one by one, on the spot, so that she couldn't lapse into her undisciplined spending habits.

Finally, I loaned her $1,500 against her year-end bonus, which she would be receiving within two months, so that she could get her car back.

The point I want to emphasize is this: which do you think was most important to this woman when it came down to the wire: the

The Challenge

couple hundred thousand dollars she had made and spent over the years or the $55,000 she had been able to save?

I was especially able to identify with this woman's plight because I, too, had considered killing myself when I owed my quarter-million dollars. It was only through talking to Abe that I was able to face my problem and plot a way out of it. Abe taught me the necessity of having a financial net worth before I could have a personal self-worth.

I tell you this story only because if you're going to move forward with your life, you'll have to put behind you the issues that are binding you to your past.

Okay. Now it's your turn.

I'm asking you to invest the next hour in making your life substantially better. Pick out those top three things—you know what they are without even thinking—swallow hard, go to work, and get them behind you.

Call your biggest creditor. Tell him you want to pay but just don't have the money. Call the IRS. Tell them there must be some misunderstanding but you want to get it straightened out. Call in that longtime employee and let him know that you've got to let him go. He already knows it. The both of you will sleep better tonight.

You need to get past your past so that you can focus all of your resources on building your future.

And that brings me, reluctantly, to the end of this book. You will recall at its beginning that I told you I had a pact with Abe to share with you some of the principles he had taught me during our summer together on the beach, and I hope I've fulfilled that promise. I'd like to close this book as I close some of my speeches with, of course, one more story:

It is about an eight-year-old boy who approaches an old man in front of a wishing well, looks up into his eyes, and begins:

"I understand you're the wisest man in the world, and I'd like to know the secret of life."

The old man looks down at the youngster and replies, "I don't think I'm the wisest man in the world, but I think I have thought a lot during my lifetime, and I think the secret can be wrapped up in four words:

"The first word is *think*. Think about the values you wish to live your life by.

"The second word, little boy, is *believe*. Believe in yourself based on the thinking you've done about the values you're going to live your life by.

"The third word, little boy, is *dream*. Dream about the things that can be, based on the belief in yourself, based on thinking you've done about the values you're going to live your life by.

"And the fourth word, little boy, is *dare*. Dare to make your dreams become reality, based on the belief in yourself, and the thinking you've done about the values you're going to live your life by."

And with that, Walter E. Disney said to the little boy, "**Think, Believe, Dream,** and **Dare.**"

Index

Index